W9-BYH-847

SECOND EDITION / CD INCLUDED

Christian Weddings

Resources to Make Your Ceremony Unique

Andy Langford

Abingdon Press
Nashville

Christian Weddings

Library of Congress Cataloging-in-Publication Data

Langford, Andy.
  Christian weddings / Andy Langford. -- 2nd ed.
    p. cm.
  ISBN 978-0-687-64959-4 (binding: adhesive pbk. with cd insert : alk. paper)
  1. Marriage service. 2. Weddings. I. Title.

  BV199.M3L36 2008
  265'.5--dc22

Copyright page continued on pages 92–93.

08 09 10 11 12 13 14 15 16 17—10 9 8 7 6 5 4 3 2 1
MANUFACTURED IN THE UNITED STATES OF AMERICA

To my wife, Sally, who planned our own wedding with me;
our daughter Ann Green Langford Duncan and her husband, Nathan;
and our daughter Sarah Overby Langford
and the man she will someday marry

Contents

Introduction: How to Make Your Wedding Your Own
Unique Ceremony vii

1. Gathering 1

2. Greeting 4

3. Charge to the Man and Woman 16

4. Declaration of Intention or Consent 19

5. Presentation 22

6. Response of the Families, Children, and Congregation 24

7. Opening Prayer 29

8. Hymns and Special Music 34

9. Scripture Lessons, Psalms, and Poetry 37

10. Homily 40

11. Intercessory Prayer 41

12. Exchange of Vows 47

13. Taking, Blessing, and Exchanging of Rings 54

14. Unity Candle 60

15. Declaration of Marriage 62

16. Blessing of the Marriage 65

17. The Lord's Prayer 77

18. Thanksgiving and Holy Communion 79

19. Dismissal with Blessing 86

20. Introduction of the Couple 90

Acknowledgments 92

Additional CD-ROM Contents

Appendix A: Wedding Service Worksheet

Appendix B: Wedding Planning Questionnaire

Appendix C: Sample Wedding Bulletin

INTRODUCTION
How to Make Your Wedding Your Own Unique Ceremony

The Holy Bible opens with the first man, Adam, speaking about the first woman, Eve: "This is now bone of my bones and flesh of my flesh; / she shall be called 'woman,' for she was taken out of man" (Genesis 2:23 TNIV). Immediately, the biblical author describes the first sacred covenant recorded in Scripture: "For this reason a man will leave his father and mother and be united to his wife, and they will become one flesh" (Genesis 2:24 TNIV).

Ever since creation, men and women have come together in this sacred bond that we now call marriage. *Christian Weddings: Resources to Make Your Ceremony Unique* helps celebrate this covenant in ways that are both holy and particular to every wedding couple.

This book is for you if you are

- a couple planning your own wedding
- a pastor desiring wedding resources from a variety of Christian traditions
- a couple coming from different Christian worship traditions
- a pastor assisting a couple in planning their wedding

A Christian wedding is a sacred covenant in which a man and a woman commit themselves to live together among other followers of Jesus Christ. The worship service enacts a series of symbolic events that represent how each member of the couple feels about the other and how they will act toward each other in their new life together. Just as important, a wedding is a solemn and public union that is blessed by God, the church universal, and a community of family and friends. How does all this happen in just a few minutes on the wedding day?

William Shakespeare described a Christian wedding (*Twelfth Night* 5.1.159–164). In just six lines, Shakespeare outlined the basic marriage service still used by many Christian couples today:

> A contract of eternal bond of love,
> Confirm'd by mutual joinder of your hands,
> Attested by the holy close of lips,
> Strength'ned by interchangement of your rings,
> And all the ceremony of this compact
> Seal'd in my function, by my testimony.

The Anglo-Saxon word *wedd*, the source of our modern word *wedding*, originally meant to gamble or wager. Essentially, a groom made a financial pledge to a bride's father betting that the bride would be a faithful companion and give birth to healthy children. While some marriages today seem designed for media coverage or social enhancement, Christian couples enter marriage expecting a lifelong and total commitment to each other. This book helps make the service of Christian marriage not a bet or social affair but a sacred covenant.

This sacred covenant is also a legal contract. For example, the book *You and the Law* (edited by Henry Poor [Pleasantville, N.Y.: Reader's Digest, 1984], 365) states:

> In the eyes of the law marriage is a contract whereby a man and a woman agree to enter into a union for life for their mutual benefit, to provide each other with companionship, sexual gratification and economic help and to procreate and raise children. The fact that none of these considerations may be mentioned at the time of marriage doesn't make them any the less binding. They are inherent in the marital contract. Many of them result from customs and religious doctrines that are almost 2,000 years old and have been incorporated into present-day laws by both our legislatures and our courts.

Christian weddings acknowledge this legal recognition of mutual responsibilities, yet understand marriage to be much more so a sacred bond. How do we acknowledge this holy covenant in the ceremony itself?

This book collects the finest available Christian marriage resources from almost thirty major Christian worship traditions in the English-speaking world. While some couples and pastors prefer to write their own services, many times they do not have the acquired ability to prepare the right liturgy. The test of time and experience commend these resources to us as the best available words, signs, and actions to make each ceremony a holy moment.

These words, signs, and actions clearly testify that the ceremony is a Christian marriage. These resources, however, are only effective when truly affirmed by each partner as his or her personal witness. To make each ceremony more specific to an individual couple, the partners have the freedom to amend these resources to reflect their own understandings of the marriage covenant. Each marriage service should reflect the values and beliefs shared by the couple.

Marriage services today demand such a rich collection. Bonds of love between couples have taken precedence over bonds of faith, ethnicity, race, and region. Unlike in previous generations, today Roman Catholics are marrying Baptists, United Methodists are marrying Episcopalians, Scottish Presbyterians are marrying Canadian Anglicans, and the list continues. Marriage between persons of different Christian traditions is the contemporary way. This book works exceptionally well in all these situations and many more.

Interfaith weddings, however, which involve a Christian partner with a person of another faith such as Judaism or Islam or Hinduism, pose very different concerns. An interfaith service may be conducted by a religious leader from one tradition, or several religious leaders working together. The difficulty in many interfaith weddings is that a number of religious traditions today refuse to sanction such interfaith services. Currently, many rabbis refuse to participate in a wedding when one of the partners is not Jewish. Most Roman Catholic priests will not participate in weddings that involve a non–Roman Catholic partner. Within some Christian traditions, clergy will not participate in a service that involves a person who has been divorced or has not met particular religious criteria. The issue of same-sex relationships, now called marriages in some states, makes the wedding landscape even more complex.

Yet despite all these difficulties, interfaith marriages and diverse Christian unions take place frequently. These services may simply involve a secular wedding with signs from each of the religious traditions. In these cases, the first step must be an honest conversation with the secular or religious leaders who may be asked to participate in the wedding. Because of many challenges, resources out of non-Christian religious traditions are not included in this book, but may be found in the prayer books of the other traditions. For a ceremony in which one partner is a Christian, the resources included in this book provide a good starting point for planning an interfaith wedding service.

Who plans a Christian wedding? A minister, pastor, or priest (called throughout this book "pastor") usually presides at a service of Christian marriage. Typically, the couple chooses a pastor with whom both partners feel comfortable as they prepare to plan their special ceremony.

In addition to giving premarital counseling and honoring the requirements of a congregation or tradition, the pastor typically leads in designing the marriage service with both the bride and the groom. The decision to perform the ceremony is the right and responsibility of the pastor, in accordance with the laws of the state and the particular denomination.

At times, the pastor may be obligated to respect and honor the policies of a congregation or denomination rather than the wishes of the couple. In the premarital counseling, the pastor informs the couple of policies or guidelines established by the congregation (if the service is held in church facilities) on such matters as particular worship options, worship decorations, photography, and audio or video recording. By tradition, any other clergy involved in the wedding should be invited by the presiding pastor of the church where the service is held. Ultimately, the pastor in charge should approve the final plans for the wedding service.

Within this context, however, the couple should, in conversation with the pastor, trust their own instincts and make clear decisions about what will be the best wedding ceremony for them. Traditionally, the bride and the groom are the ministers of the service because they alone are creating the new covenant between them. The pastor serves as a witness and presider, similar to the role of a lawyer at the sale of a piece of property. The pastor does not "marry the couple"; technically, the bride and the groom marry each other. The pastor ensures that the covenant created is both sacred and lawful. There is no one right way or wrong way to be united in Christian marriage. Make this service unique to the specific couple!

The words and actions in all these resources consistently reflect the belief that husband and wife are equal partners in Christian marriage and that they are entering into the marriage of their own free will. The wedding, despite the tendencies of some grooms to let the brides make these plans, ideally is not planned by one partner without the input and insights of the other.

Every wedding will be a beautiful experience. Be careful not to worry about every detail or expect that everything will be perfect. A wedding may be a large, elaborate affair in a cathedral or a simple, private service in a living room. Hundreds of people can be involved or just a pastor and witnesses. All Christian weddings, however, are a special service of holy worship. Essential elements are the love between the couple, their commitment to each other, and their desire to have God as part of their relationship. Everything else about Christian marriage is secondary.

The basic outline of a Christian wedding is held in common by most churches, and this book's outline follows this structure (see the contents, pages v–vi, for this outline) that may include up to twenty distinctive movements. Shakespeare got it right, however, when he listed four key acts around which every other sign revolves: the exchange of vows, the holding of hands, the exchange of rings, and a kiss. Whenever the couple or pastor believes changes are appropriate, it is quite possible to change this basic outline.

Christian weddings may be held in many settings. From a cathedral to a chapel in the woods, from a hotel ballroom to a beach, from a living room in a home to a mountaintop, from a tent in a backyard to a sailboat on a lake— all are appropriate for a Christian wedding. While many couples continue to be married in the bride's home congregation, couples increasingly choose a location convenient for all members of the wedding party or a "destination wedding" in a special location.

Wherever the wedding takes place, the couple should be alert that the setting not detract from the Christian character of the service itself. For example, does it really witness to God if the pastor is dressed like Elvis or Santa Claus (as sometimes happens!)? A service in a sanctuary of a local congregation often dictates many aspects of the service. For example, a congregation with a central aisle lends itself to a different style of processional entrance than a worship center with side aisles. Be clear how the ceremony must adapt to the setting.

One aspect of a wedding setting that suggests special attention is the central altar or table where the bride and groom gather for the heart of the service. This setting may simply include a cross, candles, or flowers. Other table settings are possible: a candle or candles to remember a deceased parent or family member, an object that is special to the couple, a picture that is unique to the couple, samples of soil or water representing the various places from which the families come, or a loaf of bread and cup for Holy

Communion. Another option is that members of the entire congregation or representatives of each family place on the central table other signs that may bless the marriage.

The guests at a wedding should be an active congregation rather than simply passive witnesses. These resources encourage the congregation to give their blessing to the couple. The congregation may also sing hymns, join in prayer, and participate through other acts of worship.

To assist the congregation to participate in the service, a wedding bulletin provides not only a memory of this special day but often invites guests to assist fully in the ceremony. (See appendix C for a "Sample Wedding Bulletin.")

Any children of the man or the woman, other family members, and friends may take a variety of roles in the service, depending on their ages and abilities. These family members and friends may, for example, be members of the wedding party, participate in the Response of the Families and Children, read Scripture lessons, sing or play instrumental music, or make a witness in their own words. A young child from a previous marriage may be embraced by both partners before being seated with a family member. As families become more diverse, carefully involve as many members of the families as possible.

The role of younger children, however, may detract from a wedding. If a child becomes restless or loses focus, the attention of the congregation shifts from the couple to the child. Generally, it is best that when younger children are involved, they participate early in the service, such as distributing flowers on the aisle, and then be seated with a responsible adult or taken to a nursery.

Persons who have had second or even more marriages may also find valuable resources in this book. Often, disparate families are merged in a new marriage. Persons who have been married previously understand the difficulty of marriage and the deep pain experienced when marriage ends by either divorce or death. Realism balances naïveté. Because of the unique situations, each of the elements of the services may be amended to make each act of worship appropriate to the couple.

When older persons choose to marry, the wedding has much significance for the couple and their extended families. Many times, at least one partner may have lost a longtime spouse. In these situations, the couple may adapt the relevant parts of the service to ensure that the liturgy speaks clearly for them. Adult children and other members of the families may also participate in various ways to bless the marriage.

The organist or person in charge of the music should be consulted and work with the couple in all decisions on music selection. The service will be quite different depending on whether the primary instrument is a pipe organ or a hammered dulcimer or a praise band. The wedding hymns listed in this book are a starting place for choosing congregational music.

The music dramatically affects the mood of the service. The couple and music director should carefully choose all the congregational and instrumental music to reflect the tastes of the couple and to witness to the Christian nature of the service. Music may be incorporated at many places throughout the ceremony. Working together, the pastor and the musician along with the couple can easily design a unified service.

Ethnic and cultural traditions are wonderful and may be incorporated into the service. For example, Hispanics have a tradition of the couple wearing a large loop of rosary beads, placed in a figure-eight shape around the necks of the man and the woman after they say their vows. Spend some time in the planning to discover any special wedding traditions that are unique to the couple or their families.

A wedding director is helpful in assisting during a larger wedding. The director, however, is not in charge of the service itself! The director should have a copy of the service prepared by the pastor and couple, and then guide all the participants through the service. It is especially helpful for the director to have a copy of the service before the rehearsal, but the pastor should be the one to direct the service during rehearsal.

One issue that sometimes causes problems is the role of persons taking photographs and videos of the wedding. Pastors and congregations often have policies that limit the use of photography during the actual service in a church sanctuary. Such policies are intended to preserve the sanctity of the marriage without interrupting the service with flash photography or a moving photographer. Discuss this issue of photography in the planning sessions.

The appendices included on the CD-ROM that accompanies this book will make this resource even more useful.

The "Wedding Service Worksheet" (appendix A) is an outline of the wedding ceremony with spaces for a couple to mark their choices and decisions. The couple will give a completed copy of this worksheet, or the worksheet and a copy of this book itself with marks and changes throughout, to the pastor, and then they together may discuss the service. This outline also helps the pastor print out a copy of the service for everyone to use on the wedding day.

The "Wedding Planning Questionnaire" (appendix B) provides an additional resource that will be essential at the rehearsal and wedding itself. The couple and wedding director should work on this document together. Every decision made in advance is one less decision to make at the rehearsal or on the day of the wedding.

The "Sample Wedding Bulletin" (appendix C) is a sample bulletin that the couple may use in designing their own bulletin.

Use these three resources throughout the planning. After printing out each of these worksheets from the enclosed CD-ROM, use a pencil to fill them in; plans will change!

This resource does not include details about the many other arrangements necessary for a wedding, such as flowers, banners, a wedding reception, a rehearsal dinner/party, and the other items involved. A number of persons and other fine resources will assist the couple in making these plans.

Sometimes, many other aspects of the wedding seem to take precedence over the actual worship service itself. For example, in the delightful movie *Father of the Bride*, the actual worship service occupies only a few minutes. Remember, the service of Christian worship is the center of the wedding day!

Be careful that the amount and cost of the extras at a service reflect the values of the couple and not the needs of our consumerist society. Weddings have become a big business. Watch *Father of the Bride* if you do not believe this observation. Many couples are encouraged to add many elements to the wedding to make it elegant, glamorous, romantic, or perfect. Avoid the strong temptation to give in to this marketing. The heart of the marriage service is the ceremony itself, not the flowers, candles, video shots, photographs, modes of transportation, and reception. Keep the focus on the marriage covenant itself in all planning.

Finally, print a copy of the wedding ceremony and keep the service with the marriage license. On the anniversary of the wedding, the couple may read the service again to remember the vows made and blessings received. This activity is a renewal of the service that will strengthen the marriage. Someday, the couple may even decide to make a public reaffirmation of their marriage using an adaptation of the ceremony from their wedding day.

The resources in this book include the major recent services of Christian marriage of English-speaking churches around the world. Although not every word of every service is included, this book offers the most distinctive contributions of each tradition. The various resources are identified by abbreviated names:

African Methodist Episcopal is the Solemnization of Matrimony I of the *African Methodist Episcopal Church Book of Worship*. It was published in 1984 by this predominantly African American denomination.

Alternatives comes from *Wedding Alternatives*, a 1990s resource of socially responsible wedding ideas, published by the nondenominational publishing unit, Alternatives.

Australian is the Marriage Service of the Uniting Church in Australia, found in the 1988 *Uniting in Worship*. This is the dominant Protestant denomination in Australia. The spelling of words has been changed to conform to usage in the United States.

Baptist includes resources from Baptist congregations throughout the United States, found in *The Wedding Collection* by Morris H. Chapman (1991) and published by Broadman Press. Some changes are made to make the language more inclusive.

British Methodist is the Marriage Service of the 1975 *Methodist Service Book* of the British Methodist Conference. It is a contemporary updating of services unique to the Wesleyan tradition.

Canadian Anglican is the Marriage Service of *The Book of Alternative Services* of the Anglican Church of Canada, published in 1985. This is an alternative service book to the traditional Anglican *Book of Common Prayer*.

Celtic includes several prayers from *Celtic Daily Prayer: Prayers and Readings from the Northumbria Community* of 2002. These texts include ancient Celtic prayers from northern England that have been updated for modern worship.

Church of England 1980 is the Marriage Service of *The Alternative Service Book* for use in the Church of England, published in 1980. It is a contemporary updating of the classic *Book of Common Prayer*. The spelling of words has been changed to conform to usage in the United States.

Church of England 2000 is the Marriage Service of the *Services and Prayers of the Church of England Common Prayer*. It is a further updating of *The Book of Common Prayer*. The spelling of words has been changed to conform to usage in the United States.

Church of Scotland is the First Order for the Celebration of Marriage from *The Book of Common Order* of 1979 of the Church of Scotland.

Church of South India is the Marriage Service from the Church of South India of 1962 as found in *The Church of South India Book of Common Worship*. This was one of the first contemporary worship books.

Ecumenical comes from the 1987 *A Christian Celebration of Marriage: An Ecumenical Liturgy* of the North American Consultation on Common Texts, a group of leading worship experts from many traditions in the United States and Canada.

Episcopal, from 1979, is a Celebration and Blessing of a Marriage from *The Book of Common Prayer* according to the use in the Episcopal Church in the United States. This service is the basis of many wedding resources throughout the United States.

Evangelical Covenant is the Rite of Marriage II from *The Covenant Book of Worship* of the Evangelical Covenant Church of America, published in 1981.

Evangelical United Brethren is a traditional text from the ritual of the Evangelical United Brethren Church found in *The Book of Ritual of the Evangelical United Brethren Church*, published in 1959. This church was one of the predecessors of The United Methodist Church.

Lutheran 1978 is the Marriage text from 1978 found in *The Lutheran Book of Worship* of the Lutheran Church, U.S.A., the Evangelical Lutheran Church of Canada, and the Lutheran Church—Missouri Synod.

Lutheran 2006 is the Marriage service from the 2006 *Evangelical Lutheran Worship* of the Evangelical Lutheran Church in America and the Evangelical Lutheran Church in Canada.

Methodist is a traditional United Methodist marriage service, based primarily on the 1965 service from the *Methodist Book of Worship for Church and Home*, with additions from the 1959 Evangelical United Brethren *Book of Ritual*. This service is also found in *The United Methodist Book of Worship* (1992). This church was one of the predecessors of The United Methodist Church.

Moravian is the 1995 Wedding Service of the Moravian Church, found in the *Moravian Book of Worship*.

Presbyterian is the 1993 Christian Marriage from the *Book of Common Worship* of the Presbyterian Church (U.S.A.) and the Cumberland Presbyterian Church.

Quaker comes from a private liturgy at one Quaker Society meeting.

Reformed is the 1987 Order of Worship for Christian Marriage of the Reformed Church in America, found in *Worship the Lord*.

Roman Catholic comes from the Wedding Mass of *The Sacramentary* approved for use in the Dioceses of the United States of America by the National Conference of Catholic Bishops and Confirmed by the Apostolic See. This book was published by the Liturgical Press in 1985.

Unitarian comes from a private liturgy presented at one Unitarian Universalist congregation.

United Church of Canada is the 1985 *Rite II Wedding Service* of the United Church of Canada. This church is the dominant Protestant denomination in Canada.

United Church of Christ is a 1986 Service of Marriage from the *Book of Worship of the United Church of Christ*, a contemporary service stressing the equality of the man and the woman.

United Methodist is a contemporary Service of Christian Marriage found in *The United Methodist Book of Worship*, published in 1992. This service is also found in the *1989 United Methodist Hymnal*.

May this book and its many resources help pastors and couples create a wedding service that truly honors human love and God's love for us.

CHAPTER ONE
Gathering

*W*hile *the people gather, instrumental or vocal music may be offered by soloists, small ensembles, or recorded tracks. Traditionally, the music would have included the "Wedding March" from Wagner's* Lohengrin *or Pachelbel's* Canon in D. *Today, many styles of music may be used to set the tone of the celebration. For example, church steeple bells or handbells may be rung. Here and throughout the service, while the use of music appropriate for Christian worship is strongly encouraged, all decisions finally rest in the hands of the couple, musicians, and pastor.*

This is an ideal time to include solos or other special music. For example, a solo may be sung prior to or after the seating of the bride's mother.

During the Gathering, guests and families are seated and candles lighted.

If a unity candle is used, the two side candles representing the husband and the wife are lighted first, often by the respective mothers or other members of the family, while the family is being seated at the beginning of the service. Indicate in the planning who will light which candles. In choosing candles, however, be careful. Check to see if the candle produces too much wax, is scented with a fragrance to which someone may be allergic, or even has an offensive smell, such as citronella.

Some couples may also choose to light a candle or candles to remember or honor persons who cannot be present at the wedding, such as a deceased parent or grandparent. Other items may be added by family or friends to the worship settings in the moments before the service. These items may include an object that is special to the couple, a picture that is unique to the couple, samples of soil or water representing the various places from which the families come, or a loaf of bread and cup for Holy Communion. Another option is that members of the entire congregation or representatives of each family may place on the altar or table objects that may bless the marriage.

One of the most difficult of all decisions at weddings today is which family members will sit where. Traditionally, the groom's family sits on the right side facing the pastor, while the bride's family sits on the left side facing the pastor. More specifically, the groom's mother (or parents) sits on the first row. The bride's mother sits alone on the opposite first row until joined by the father of the bride, who sits with her after the Presentation.

But what happens when the couple's parents or grandparents and other family members who are all present for the wedding have been divorced or remarried? Where will the children of previous marriages sit? Every participant must remember that this day is a day to honor the couple and not a day to pull rank or revive old wounds. The couple and their families must spend some time in prayerful consideration before the rehearsal to decide who will sit where and with whom in ways that honor everyone and prevent possible conflicts.

Before, during, or immediately after the entrance of the wedding party, there may be a hymn, a psalm, a canticle (a song from Scripture), a contemporary song, or an anthem. The congregation may be invited to stand. The following processional hymns may be found in a variety of hymnals:

"All Creatures of Our God and King"
"All Praise to Thee, for Thou, O King Divine"
"Amazing Grace"
"Blest Are They"
"Christ Is Made the Sure Foundation"
"Come Down, O Love Divine"
"Come, My Way, My Truth, My Life"
"Come, Thou Almighty King"
"Come, We That Love the Lord"
"For the Beauty of the Earth"
"God of Our Life"
"Hear Us Now, Our God"
"How Can We Name a Love"
"In Thee Is Gladness"
"Jesus, Joy of Our Desiring"
"Joyful, Joyful, We Adore Thee"
"Let All the World in Every Corner Sing"
"Let's Sing to the Lord / Cantemos al Señor"
"Lord of All Hopefulness"
"Love Divine, All Loves Excelling"
"O God, Our Help in Ages Past"

"O Perfect Love"
"O Young and Fearless Prophet"
"Praise, My Soul, the King of Heaven"
"Praise the Lord Who Reigns Above"
"Praise to the Lord, the Almighty"
"Sing Praise to God Who Reigns Above"
"The King of Love My Shepherd Is"
"Where Charity and Love Prevail"
"Where Love Is Found"
"Ye Watchers and Ye Holy Ones"
"Your Love, O God, Has Called Us Here"

The wedding party enters at this time. Typically, the order of the entrance of the wedding party follows this pattern: the groom's grandparents, the bride's grandparents, the groom's parents, and finally the bride's mother. The wedding party follows: pastor(s), groom, best man, groomsmen, bridesmaids, maid of honor (unmarried woman) or matron of honor (married woman), ring bearer, and flower girl(s). See the "Wedding Planning Questionnaire" (appendix B) to outline the order of the procession and to be clear about who is escorting whom.

The way the couple enters says much about their relationship to each other and their relationship to their family members. Think carefully about the entrance of the bride and groom.

Traditionally, when the entire wedding party is in place, the bride and her father or male member of her family enter. Alternatively, the woman and the man may enter individually or together. Or the woman and the man may both be escorted by representatives of their families (traditionally, the groom by his father or best man, and the bride by her father or other male family member) until they have reached the pastor, or through the Response of the Families, at which time their escorts are seated.

CHAPTER TWO
Greeting

The Greeting, an invitation to worship by the pastor facing the congregation that is seated, introduces the couple and congregation to the nature of Christian marriage and welcomes the congregation. This time often includes the biblical witness about marriage, such as Jesus' first miracle, his participation in the wedding at Cana of Galilee when Jesus turned water into wine. According to the tradition of the Church of South India, the man and woman place garlands of flowers on each other following the Greeting.

The first words of Greeting may be a brief scriptural preface. Choose one of the following three scriptural greetings or one of the additional greetings.

2.1

I will sing of your steadfast love, O LORD, forever;
  with my mouth I will proclaim your faithfulness to all generations.
I declare that your steadfast love is established forever;
  your faithfulness is as firm as the heavens.

Psalm 89:1-2

2.2

Praise the LORD!
  Praise the name of the LORD!
  give praise, O servants of the LORD,
you that stand in the house of the LORD,
  in the courts of the house of our God.
Praise the LORD, for the LORD is good;
  sing to [the Lord's] name, for [the Lord] is gracious.

Psalm 135:1-3

2.3

God is love, and those who abide in love
   abide in God, and God abides in them.   1 John 4:16

This is the day that the LORD has made;
   let us rejoice and be glad in it.   Psalm 118:24

O give thanks, to the LORD, for he is good;
   for his steadfast love endures forever.   Psalm 106:1

2.4

Love comes from God.
   Everyone who truly loves is a child of God.
Let us worship God.   (United Church of Christ)

2.5

Friends, we are gathered together in the sight of God
to witness and bless the joining together
     of *Groom's Name* and *Bride's Name*
   in Christian marriage.
The covenant of marriage was established by God,
   who created us male and female for each other.
With his presence and power
   Jesus graced a wedding at Cana of Galilee,
and in his sacrificial love
   gave us the example for the love of husband and wife.
Groom's Name and *Bride's Name* come to give themselves
     to one another
   in this holy covenant.   (United Methodist)

2.6

Dearly beloved,
we are gathered together here in the sight of God,
   and in the presence of these witnesses,
   to join together this man and this woman
     (*Groom's Name* and *Bride's Name*)

in holy matrimony,
which is an honorable estate, instituted of God,
   and signifying unto us
   the mystical union that exists between Christ and his Church;
which holy estate Christ adorned and beautified
   with his presence in Cana of Galilee.
It is therefore not to be entered into unadvisedly,
   but reverently, discreetly, and in the fear of God.
Into this holy estate these two persons come now to be joined.

(Methodist)

2.7

The grace of our Lord Jesus Christ, the love of God,
   and the communion of the Holy Spirit be with you all.

And also with you.

Let us pray.
Eternal God, our creator and redeemer,
   as you gladdened the wedding at Cana in Galilee
   by the presence of your Son,
so by his presence now bring your joy to this wedding.
Look in favor upon *Groom's Name* and *Bride's Name*
   and grant that they, rejoicing in all your gifts,
     may at length celebrate with Christ the marriage feast
      which has no end. **Amen.**

(Lutheran 1978)

2.8

The grace of our Lord Jesus Christ, the love of God,
   and the communion of the Holy Spirit be with you all.

And also with you.

Let us pray.
Gracious God, you sent your Son Jesus Christ

into the world to reveal your love to all people.
Enrich *Groom's Name* and *Bride's Name* with every good gift,
that their life together may show forth your love;
and grant that at the last we may all celebrate with Christ
the marriage feast that has no end;
in the name of Jesus Christ our Lord. Amen.

(Lutheran 2006)

2.9

Dearly beloved:
We have come together in the presence of God
to witness and bless
the joining together of this man and this woman
in Holy Matrimony.
The bond and covenant of marriage
was established by God in creation,
and our Lord Jesus Christ adorned this manner of life
by his presence and first miracle
at a wedding in Cana of Galilee.
It signifies to us the mystery of the union
between Christ and his Church,
and Holy Scripture commends it
to be honored among all people.
The union of husband and wife in heart, body, and mind
is intended by God for their mutual joy,
for the help and comfort given one another
in prosperity and adversity;
and when it is God's will, for the procreation of children
and their nurture in the knowledge and love of the Lord.
Therefore marriage is not to be entered into
unadvisedly or lightly,
but reverently, deliberately,
and in accordance with the purposes
for which it was instituted by God.   (Episcopal)

2.10

Dearly beloved, we are gathered here as the people of God
   to witness the marriage of *Groom's Name* and *Bride's Name*.
We come to share in their joy and to ask God to bless them.
Marriage is a gift of God, sealed by a sacred covenant.
God gives human love.
Through that love, husband and wife
   come to know each other with mutual care and companionship.
God gives joy.
Through that joy, wife and husband may share their new
     life with others
   as Jesus shared new wine at the wedding in Cana.
With our love and our prayers,
   we support *Groom's Name* and *Bride's Name*
   as they now freely give themselves to each other.

(United Church of Christ)

2.11

Dear friends, we have come together in the presence of God
   to witness the marriage of *Groom's Name* and *Bride's Name*,
   to surround them with our prayers, and to share in their joy.
The scriptures teach us that the bond and covenant
     of marriage is a gift of God,
   a holy mystery in which man and woman become one flesh,
   an image of the union of Christ and the church.
As this woman and this man
     give themselves to each other today,
   we remember that at Cana in Galilee
   our Savior Jesus Christ made the wedding feast
     a sign of God's reign of love.
Let us enter into this celebration confident
     that through the Holy Spirit,
Christ is present with us now.
We pray that this couple may fulfill God's purpose
     for the whole of their lives.

(United Church of Christ)

2.12

We gather in the presence of God
   to give thanks for the gift of marriage,
   to witness the joining together
     of *Groom's Name* and *Bride's Name*,
   to surround them with our prayers,
and to ask God's blessing upon them,
   so that they may be strengthened for their life together
   and nurtured in their love for God.
God created us male and female, and gave us marriage
   so that husband and wife may help and comfort each other,
   living faithfully together in plenty and in want,
   in joy and in sorrow, in sickness and in health,
   throughout all their days.
God gave us marriage
   for the full expression of the love
     between a man and a woman.
In marriage a woman and a man belong to each other,
   and with affection and tenderness
     freely give themselves to each other.
God gave us marriage for the well-being of human society,
   for the ordering of family life,
and for the birth and nurture of children.
God gave us marriage as a holy mystery
   in which a man and a woman are joined together,
and become one, just as Christ is one with the church.
In marriage, husband and wife are called to a new way of life,
   created and ordered, and blessed by God.
This way of life must not be entered into carelessly,
   or from selfish motives, but responsibly, and prayerfully.
We rejoice that marriage is given by God,
   blessed by our Lord Jesus Christ,
   and sustained by the Holy Spirit.
Therefore, let marriage be held in honor by all.   (Presbyterian)

2.13

Marriage is appointed by God.

The church believes that marriage is a gift of God in creation
and a means of grace in which man and woman
become one in heart, mind, and body.

Marriage is the sacred and lifelong union of a man and a woman
who give themselves to each other in love and trust.

It signifies the mystery of the union
between Christ and the church.

Marriage is given that husband and wife
may enrich and encourage each other
in every part of their life together.

Marriage is given that with delight and tenderness
they may know each other in love,

and through their physical union
may strengthen the union of their lives.

Marriage is given that children may be born
and brought up in security and love,
that home and family life may be strengthened,
and that society may stand upon firm foundations.

Marriage is a way of life which all people should honor;
it is not to be entered into lightly or selfishly,
but responsibly and in the love of God.

Groom's Name and *Bride's Name* are now to begin
this way of life
which God has created and Christ has blessed.

Therefore, on this their wedding day, we pray for them,
asking that they may fulfill God's purpose for the whole
of their lives. (Australian)

2.14

Dearly beloved, we are gathered together here
in the sight of God and these witnesses,
to join together this man and this woman in the holy
estate of matrimony.

The Bible teaches that marriage was created by God.

God made a helpmate for Adam and called her woman,
	for she was taken from the man.
In the Old Testament, Moses, the lawgiver,
	gave divine sanction to marriage as a legal institution.
In the New Testament,
	the Book of Hebrews says that marriage
		is honorable among all.
Therefore, because God has put God's blessing upon this union,
	and this is a service of Christian worship
		celebrating the work of God,
	let us pause to ask for God's blessing
		and presence in this service. (Baptist)

2.15

Dear friends, we have come together in the presence of God
	to witness the marriage of *Groom's Name* and *Bride's Name*,
	and to rejoice with them.
Marriage is a gift of God and a means of his grace,
	in which man and woman become one flesh.
It is God's purpose that
	as husband and wife give themselves to each other in love,
	they shall grow together and be united in that love,
	as Christ is united with his Church.
The union of man and woman in heart, body, and mind
	is intended for their mutual comfort and help,
	that they may know each other with delight and
		tenderness in acts of love
(and that they may be blessed
	in the procreation, care, and upbringing of children).
In marriage, husband and wife give themselves to each other,
	to care for each other in good times and in bad.
They are linked to each other's families,
	and they begin a new life together in the community.
It is a way of life that all should reverence,
	and none should lightly undertake. (Canadian Anglican)

2.16

Christian marriage is a joyful covenanting between a man and a woman
  in which they proclaim, before God and human witnesses,
    their commitment to live together
      in spiritual, physical, and material unity.
In this covenant
    they acknowledge that the great love
      God has shown for each of them
    enables them to love each other.
They affirm that God's gracious presence and abiding power
    are needed for them to keep their vows,
      to continue to live in love,
    and to be faithful servants of Christ in this world.
For human commitment is fragile and human love imperfect,
    but the promise of God is eternal
    and the love of God can bring our love to perfection.

(Reformed)

2.17

Unless the Lord builds the house,
  its builders will have toiled in vain.
Our help is in the Name of the Lord,
  Maker of heaven and earth.
Beloved, we have come together in the house of God
  to celebrate the marriage of this man and this woman,
  in the assurance that the Lord Jesus Christ,
    whose power was revealed at the wedding in Cana of Galilee,
  is present with us here in all his power and his love.
Marriage is provided by God
    as part of God's loving purpose for humanity
  since the beginning of creation.
Jesus said, "The Creator made them from the beginning
      male and female.
For this reason a man shall leave his father and mother,
  and be made one with his wife:
and the two shall become one flesh."

Marriage is enriched by God
     for all who have faith in the Gospel,
   for through the saving grace of Christ
   and the renewal of the Holy Spirit
   husband and wife can love one another as Christ loves them.
Marriage is thus a gift and calling of God
   and is not to be undertaken lightly or from selfish motives
   but with reverence and dedication,
   with faith in the enabling power of Christ,
   and with due awareness of the purpose for which
     it is appointed by God.
Marriage is appointed that there may be lifelong
     companionship,
   comfort and joy between husband and wife.
It is appointed as the right and proper setting
   for the full expression of physical love
     between man and woman.
It is appointed for the ordering of family life,
   where children—who are also God's gifts to us—
   may enjoy the security of love and the heritage of faith.
It is appointed for the well-being of human society,
   which can be stable and happy only
where the marriage bond is honored and upheld.

(Church of Scotland)

2.18

Marriage is a gift of God in creation
   through which husband and wife
     grow together in love and trust,
they shall be united with one another in heart, body, and mind,
   as Christ is united with his bride, the Church.
The gift of marriage brings husband and wife together
   in the delight and tenderness of sexual union
   and joyful commitment to the end of their lives.

It is given as the foundation of family life
   in which children are (born and) nurtured
and in which each member of the family,
   in good times and in bad,
may find strength, companionship, and comfort,
   and grow to maturity in love.
Marriage is a way of life made holy by God,
   and blessed by the presence of our Lord Jesus Christ
   with those celebrating a wedding at Cana in Galilee.
Marriage is a sign of unity and loyalty
   which all should uphold and honor.
It enriches society and strengthens community.
No one should enter into it lightly or selfishly
   but reverently and responsibly in the sight of almighty God.
Groom's Name and *Bride's Name* are now
      to enter this way of life.
They will each give their consent to the other
   and make solemn vows,
   and in token of this they will each give and receive a ring.
We pray with them that the Holy Spirit will guide
   and strengthen them,
that they may fulfill God's purposes
   for the whole of their earthly life together.

(Church of England 2000)

2.19

We have come together in the presence of God,
   to witness the marriage of *Groom's Name* and *Bride's Name*,
to ask his blessing on them,
   and to share in their joy.
Our Lord Jesus Christ was himself a guest
      at a wedding in Cana in Galilee,
   and through his Spirit he is with us now.
The Bible teaches us that marriage is a gift of God in creation
   and a means of his grace,
   a holy mystery in which man and woman become one flesh.

It is God's purpose that,
    as husband and wife give themselves to each other
        in love throughout their lives,
they shall be united in that love
        as Christ is united with his Church.
Marriage is given,
    that husband and wife may comfort and help each other,
living faithfully together in need and in plenty,
    in sorrow and in joy.
It is given,
    that with delight and tenderness
        they may know each other in love,
and through the joy of their bodily union,
    may strengthen the union of their hearts and lives.
It is given as the foundation of family life
    in which children may be born and nurtured
        in accordance with God's will,
to his praise and glory.
In marriage husband and wife belong to one another,
    and they begin a new life together in the community.
It is a way of life that all should honor;
    and it must not be undertaken carelessly, lightly, or selfishly,
but reverently, responsibly, and after serious thought.
This is the way of life, created and hallowed by God,
    that *Groom's Name* and *Bride's Name* are now to begin.
They will each give their consent to the other;
    they will join hands and exchange solemn vows,
and in token to this they will each give and receive a ring.
Therefore, on this their wedding day
    we pray with them, that,
strengthened and guided by God,
    they may fulfill his purpose
for the whole of their earthly life together.

                        (Church of England 2000)

CHAPTER THREE
Charge to the Man and Woman

As the couple stands before the pastor, the pastor addresses the couple and asks about their free and mutual decision to marry. The Charge typically reminds the couple about the serious and holy nature of the marriage covenant.

3.1
I ask you now, in the presence of God and these people,
to declare your intention
to enter into union with each other
through the grace of Jesus Christ,
  who calls you into union with himself
  as acknowledged in your baptism.   (United Methodist)

3.2
I require and charge you both,
  as you stand in the presence of God,
  before whom the secrets of all hearts are disclosed,
  that, having duly considered the holy covenant
    you are about to make,
  you do now declare before this company your pledge of faith,
    each to the other.
Be well assured that if these solemn vows are kept inviolate,
  as God's Word demands,
  and if steadfastly you endeavor to do
    the will of your heavenly Father,
God will bless your marriage,
  will grant you fulfillment in it,
  and will establish your home in peace.   (Methodist)

3.3

I charge you both, as you stand in the presence of God,
    to remember that love and loyalty alone will avail
        as the foundation of a happy home.
If the solemn vows you are about to make are kept faithfully,
    and if steadfastly you endeavor to do
        the will of your heavenly Father,
your life will be full of joy,
    and the home you are establishing will abide in peace.
No other ties are more tender, no other vows more sacred
    than those you now assume.   (Evangelical United Brethren)

3.4

The Lord God in his goodness created us male and female,
    and by the gift of marriage founded human community
        in a joy that begins now and is brought to perfection
        in the life to come.
Because of sin, our age-old rebellion,
    the gladness of marriage can be overcast
and the gift of the family can become a burden.
But because God, who established marriage,
    continues still to bless it with his abundant
        and ever-present support,
we can be sustained in our weariness and have our joy restored.
Groom's Name and *Bride's Name,* if it is your intention
        to share with each other
    your joy and sorrows and all that the years will bring,
    with your promises bind yourselves to each other as husband and wife.
                                                    (Lutheran 1978)

3.5

Before God and this congregation,
    I ask you to affirm your willingness to enter
        this covenant of marriage
    and to share all the joys and sorrows of this new relationship,
    whatever the future may hold.   (United Church of Christ)

3.6

Groom's Name and *Bride's Name*,
   your marriage is intended to join you for life
   in a relationship so intimate and personal
   that it will change your whole being.
God offers you the hope, and indeed the promise,
   of a love that is true and mature.   (Evangelical Covenant)

CHAPTER FOUR
Declaration of Intention or Consent

The pastor speaks to the woman and the man individually and asks about their desire to be married and commited to each other. Traditionally, the father of the bride or her escort/presenter is still standing symbolically between the groom and the bride to ensure that each may speak honestly. The Declaration often includes the specific obligations of the man and the woman to each other. The couple should speak out their response so that the congregation may clearly hear their commitment to each other.

4.1

Name, will you have *Name* to be your husband/wife,
  to live together in holy marriage?
Will you love him/her, comfort him/her,
    honor and keep him/her,
  in sickness and in health,
and forsaking all others, be faithful to him/her
  as long as you both shall live?
Woman/man: **I will.** (United Methodist)

4.2

Name, will you have this woman/man
    to be your wedded wife/husband,
  to live together in the holy estate of matrimony?
Will you love her/him, comfort her/him,
    honor and keep her/him,
  in sickness and in health;
and forsaking all others keep only to her/him
  so long as you both shall live?
Man/woman: **I will.** (Methodist)

19

4.3

Name, will you have this man/woman to be your husband/wife;
   to live together in the covenant of marriage?
Will you love him/her, comfort him/her,
      honor and keep him/her,
   in sickness and in health;
and, forsaking all others,
   be faithful to him/her as long you both shall live?
Man/woman: **I will.**   (Episcopal)

4.4

Name, will you have *Name* to be your wife/husband,
   and will you love her/him faithfully
      as long as you both shall live?
Man/woman: **I will.**   (United Church of Christ)

4.5

Name, understanding that God has created, ordered,
   and blessed the covenant of marriage,
do you affirm your desire and intention to enter this covenant?
Man/woman: **I do.**   (Presbyterian)

4.6

*If both man and woman are baptized, the following may be
   used in addition to the above:*

Name, in your baptism
   you have been called to union with Christ and the church.
Do you intend to honor this calling
      through the covenant of marriage?
Man/woman: **I do.**   (Presbyterian)

4.7

Name, will you have this man/woman
   to be your husband/wife?
Man/woman: **I will.**   (United Church of Canada)

4.8

Do you, *Name*, now take *Name*
   to be your wife/husband;
and do you promise, in the presence of God
      and before these witnesses,
   to be a loving, faithful, and loyal husband/wife to her/him,
until God shall separate you by death?
Man/woman: **I do.**   (Church of Scotland)

4.9

Name, will you have this woman/man, *Name*,
   to be your wife/husband,
and cleave to her/him alone?
Man/woman: **I will.**   (Church of South India)

4.10

Name, do you take *Name* to be your wife/husband,
   and do you commit yourself to her/him,
to be responsible in the marriage relationship,
   to give yourself to her/him in love and work,
to invite her/him fully into your being
   so that she/he can know who you are,
to cherish her/him above all others
   and to respect her/his individuality,
   encouraging her/him to be herself/himself
and to grow in all that God intends?
Man/woman: **I do.**   (Evangelical Covenant)

CHAPTER FIVE
Presentation

---

*I*f the woman is presented (not given!) in marriage, the pastor asks the presenter(s) one of the following. Although the Presentation comes out of the ancient perspective that the woman is the property of her father, this action is often now retained as a sign of the family's blessing.

Traditionally, the presenter is the father of the bride. A brother, uncle, stepfather, godfather, or close family friend is also appropriate. In some cases, the mother of the bride may present her daughter. During a subsequent marriage, the Presentation may be made by an older or adult child from a previous marriage. It is also acceptable, however, simply for the bride to stand unaccompanied.

In some cases, both partners may be presented by a representative of each family. For example, a mother may present her son, while a father presents his daughter.

On which arm should the bride enter the worship space? Historically, the bride comes to a wedding on the left arm of her father, so that the father stands between the bride and the groom until after the Declaration of Consent and Presentation. At the Presentation, the father then joins the hands of the couple and goes to be seated. The father, however, may choose to escort in the bride on the right arm.

If the bride is wearing a veil, a sign of purity, the father or presenter removes it at the end of the Presentation.

The presenter should speak clearly so that the whole congregation hears the presenter.

5.1
If the woman is presented, the pastor asks the presenter(s):

Who presents this woman to be married to this man?
Presenter(s): **I (We) do.**   (United Methodist)

5.2
If the man is presented, the pastor asks the presenter(s):

Who presents this man to be married to this woman?
Presenter(s): **I (We) do.** (United Methodist)

5.3
If all parents wish to participate:

Groom's Name and *Bride's Name*
    have declared their intention towards each other.
As their parents,
    will you now entrust your son and daughter to one another
as they come to be married?
Parents: **We will.** (Church of England 2000)

CHAPTER SIX
Response of the Families, Children, and Congregation

*C*hristian marriage bonds not only the couple but also the whole of each of their *families*. Family members and friends have gathered to participate in the service and will be part of the larger family of the bridal couple. The following acts provide ways for both families and all the guests to participate in the worship.

One or more of the following responses by families or congregation, declaring their affirmation of the marriage, may be in place of, or in addition to, the Presentation above. If the service includes one of these Responses, print the words that the congregation may need to say in the wedding bulletin.

In addition, the groomsmen and bridesmaids are present not only to provide a visual effect but also to offer their physical, emotional, and spiritual support. Consider carefully how they may add to the service. For example, one of the wedding party may read the scripture or sing a solo, or as one group together offer words of support.

This time may also include silent meditation (a Quaker tradition), or members of the congregation may stand and offer verbal support to the couple. Because of the diversity of families and congregations, be sure to include at least one representative from each group, as possible. This time may also include brief witnesses of love and support by the family, during which particular family traditions may be remembered.

Many couples today come to a wedding with children from previous relationships. These children will be part of this marriage, and they need to participate in the creation of this new family. The wedding can be an important time to recognize these children and to let them participate and give their blessing to the marriage. These children may add their own words of blessing to the more formal statements below.

Be cautious, however, about involving children who may distract from the ceremony. Some children may be too young to participate without disrupting the service. Other children may have difficulty with the new relationship and should not be asked or forced to participate. Involve the children only when they enhance the holy moment.

6.1
Pastor to family members:

The marriage of *Groom's Name* and *Bride's Name* unites
    their families
  and creates a new one.
They ask for your blessing.

Parents and other representatives of the families may respond:

We rejoice in your union,
  and pray God's blessing upon you.   (United Methodist)

6.2
Pastor to family members:

Do you who represent their families
  rejoice in their union
and pray God's blessing upon them?

Families: **We do.**   (United Methodist)

6.3
Pastor to family members:

Will the families of *Groom's Name* and *Bride's Name*
  please stand and please answer
  in support of this couple.
Do you offer your prayerful blessing and loving support
    to this marriage?

Families: **I do.**   (United Church of Christ)

6.4
Children of the couple may repeat these or similar words, prompted line by line by the pastor:

We love both of you.
We bless your marriage.
Together we will be a family. (United Methodist)

6.5
Pastor to children of the new family:

Name, you are entering a new family.
Will you give to this new family your trust, love and affection?

Child: **I will, with the help of God.**

Pastor to bride and groom:

Groom's Name and *Bride's Name*,
    will you be faithful and loving parents
  to *Name(s) of Children?*

Couple: **We will, with the help of God.**

(United Church of Christ)

6.6
Pastor to the whole congregation:

Will all of you, by God's grace,
    do everything in your power
to uphold and care for these two persons in their marriage?

People: **We will.** (United Methodist)

6.7
The congregation may repeat the following, prompted line by line by the pastor:

May you dwell in God's presence forever;
    may true and constant love preserve you.

(Lutheran 1978)

6.8

Pastor to people:

Will all of you witnessing these promises
  do all in your power to uphold these two persons
    in their marriage?

People: **We will.**   (Episcopal)

6.9

Pastor to whole congregation:

Do you, as people of God, pledge
    your support and encouragement
  to the covenant commitment
    that *Groom's Name* and *Bride's Name*
  are making together?

People: **We do.**   (United Church of Christ)

6.10

Pastor to parents:

With gratitude for your love, support,
    and nurture through the years,
  this couple comes today to form a new family
    under God's blessing.
Do you grant to them the freedom to form a new family
  and seek God's blessing?
Do you grant them the freedom to form a new family
  and seek God's will?
Do you pledge to them your continuing love and support?
Do you promise to be quick to listen and slow to speak,
  and do you covenant to pray for them
    and the ministry God plans for them in the future?

Parents: **We do.**   (Baptist)

6.11
Pastor to families:

This couple needs the support of their families,
    for they cannot live out their vision alone.
Do you, their families,
    promise to continue to love and to nurture them,
    to keep your lives forever open to them,
that they, in turn, may love and nurture you?

Families: **We do.**   (Alternatives)

6.12
Pastor to congregation:

Do you promise to love and to nurture
    Groom's Name and *Bride's Name*,
    to be open to their friendship,
to support them and to be supported by them
    as they answer the calls of God in their marriage
        and in their ministries?

Congregation: **We do.**   (Alternatives)

CHAPTER SEVEN
Opening Prayer

The pastor or other worship leader offers a prayer to God, establishing that this wedding is a service to worship God. At this stage, the entire wedding party is in place, the couple have agreed to the marriage, and the family and congregation have blessed the marriage. Now is the time to give God's blessing to the sacred actions that follow. These prayers may also be provided in the wedding bulletin and prayed together by the whole congregation. The pastor may also include time for silent prayer for the couple.

7.1

God of all peoples,
    you are the true light illumining everyone.
You show us the way, the truth, and the life.
You love us even when we are disobedient.
You sustain us with your Holy Spirit.
We rejoice in your life in the midst of our lives.
We praise you for your presence with us,
    and especially in this act of solemn covenant;
through Jesus Christ our Lord. **Amen.** (United Methodist)

7.2

O gracious and everliving God,
    you have created us male and female in your image:
Look mercifully upon this man and this woman
    who come to you seeking your blessing,
and assist them with your grace,
    that with true fidelity and steadfast love
    they may honor and keep the promises and vows they make;
through Jesus Christ our Savior, who lives and reigns with you

in the unity of the Holy Spirit, one God, for ever and ever.
    Amen.   (Episcopal)

7.3

O God, we gather to celebrate your gift of love
    and its presence among us.
We rejoice that two people have chosen to commit themselves
    to a life of loving faithfulness to one another.
We praise you, O God,
    for the ways you have touched our lives
      with a variety of loving relationships.
We give thanks that we have experienced your love
    through the life-giving love of Jesus Christ
    and through the care and affection of other people.
At the same time, we remember and confess to you, O God,
    that we often have failed to be loving,
    that we often have taken for granted
      the people for whom we care most.
We selfishly neglect and strain the bonds
      that unite us withothers.
We hurt those who love us
      and withdraw from the community that encircles us.
Forgive us, O God.
Renew within us an affectionate spirit.
Enrich our lives with the gracious gift of your love
    so that we may embrace others with the same love.
May our participation in this celebration
      of love and commitment
    give to us a new joy and responsiveness
      to the relationship we cherish;
through Jesus Christ we pray. **Amen.**

Through the great depth and strength of God's love for us,
    God reaches out to us to forgive our sins
      and to restore us to life.

Be assured, children of God,
    that God's love enfolds us and upbuilds us
    so that we may continue to love one another
        as God has loved us.

(United Church of Christ)

7.4

Gracious God, always faithful in your love for us,
    we rejoice in your presence.
You create love. You unite us in one human family.
You offer your word and lead us in light.
You open your loving arms and embrace us with strength.
May the presence of Christ fill our hearts with new joy
    and make new the lives of your servants
        whose marriage we celebrate.
Bless all creation through this sign of your love
    shown in the love of *Groom's Name* and *Bride's Name*
        for each other.
May the power of your Holy Spirit
    sustain them and all of us in love that knows no end. **Amen.**

(United Church of Christ)

7.5

God of our mothers and of our fathers,
    hear our pledges encouraging and supporting
    this union of *Groom's Name* and *Bride's Name*.
Bless us as we offer our prayerful and loving support
        to their marriage.
Bless them as they pledge their lives to each other.
With faith in you and in each other,
    may this couple always bear witness
    to the reality of the love to which we witness this day.
May their love continue to grow,
    and may it be a true reflection of your love for us all;
through Jesus Christ. **Amen.**   (United Church of Christ)

7.6

Gracious God, you are always faithful in your love for us.
Look mercifully upon *Groom's Name* and *Bride's Name*,
  who have come seeking your blessing.
Let your Holy Spirit rest upon them
  so that with steadfast love
    they may honor the promises they make this day,
through Jesus Christ our Savior. **Amen.**   (Presbyterian)

7.7

Father, when you created humankind
  you willed that man and wife should be one.
Bind *Groom's Name* and *Bride's Name*
    in the loving union of marriage
  and make their love fruitful
  so that they may be living witnesses
    to your divine love in the world.
We ask this through our Lord Jesus Christ, your Son,
  who lives and reigns with you and the Holy Spirit,
One God, for ever and ever.   (Roman Catholic)

7.8

Loving and beloved God,
  from the beginning you have made us to live
    in partnership with one another.
We pray for the presence of your Spirit with these two persons.
Fill their hearts with sincerity and truth
  as they enter this solemn covenant. **Amen.**

(United Church of Canada)

7.9

Pastor: Friends of Christ,
  in the midst of our joy
let us also pray for this broken world.
For all people in the daily life and work;
  for our families, friends, neighbors,
and for all whose lives touch ours.

People: **We pray to you, our God.**

Pastor: For this holy fellowship of faith
  in which we seek your grace;
for the world, the nation, and this community,
  in which we work for justice, freedom, and peace.

People: **We pray to you, our God.**

Pastor: For the just and proper use of your creation;
  for the victims of hunger, injustice, and oppression.

People: **We pray to you, our God.**

Pastor: For all who are in danger, sorrow, or any kind of trouble;
  for those who minister to the sick, the friendless,
and the needy.

People: **We pray to you, our God.**

Pastor: For those who have suffered the loss of child or parent,
  husband or wife;
for those to whom love is a stranger.

People: **We pray to you, our God.**

Pastor: Most gracious God,
  you have made us in your own image
and given us over to one another's care.
Hear the prayers of your people,
  that unity may overcome division,
hope vanquish despair,
  and joy conquer sorrow.
through Jesus Christ our Lord. **Amen.**   (Ecumenical)

CHAPTER EIGHT
Hymns and Special Music

---

*T*he opening music marks the beginning of the service and sets the tone of the whole service. Consider carefully which musical instruments will be involved. An organ, piano, flute, hammered dulcimer, harp, or praise band can all be part of a service of worship. Generally, couples will plan for the opening music, closing music, and one or two pieces of music during the service. Be careful, however, not to allow the music or musicians to overwhelm the principal participants, the bride and the groom.

Many couples choose a popular song that reflects their love for each other that may be sung by a soloist or played instrumentally or through a sound system. Because of the secular nature of many of these songs, however, it often seems best that these be sung during the Gathering of the congregation and before the formal service actually begins. For example, have the soloist sing either immediately before or after the seating of the mothers. Any decisions about music should be made in consultation with the musician in charge and in accordance with the policies of the location.

During the entrance of the wedding party, there may be a hymn, a psalm, a choir anthem, a handbell anthem, a solo, or a canticle (a song from Scripture). Such music adds to the worship experience. It allows the whole congregation to participate not only with words but also with the sublime quality of music. The music provides a witness that reflects the faith and musical tastes of the couple.

Hymns in particular provide a way for the whole congregation to participate in and bless the marriage. The congregation may be invited to stand during the singing of the hymn. If the hymn is unfamiliar to some persons in the congregation, it is often useful to have a person gently lead the singing of the hymn. The following processional hymns may be found in a variety of hymnals:

"All Creatures of Our God and King"
"All Praise to Thee, for Thou, O King Divine"
"Amazing Grace"
"Blest Are Thee"
"Christ Is Made the Sure Foundation"
"Come Down, O Love Divine"
"Come, My Way, My Truth, My Life"
"Come, Thou Almighty King"
"Come, We That Love the Lord"
"For the Beauty of the Earth"
"God of Our Life"
"Hear Us Now, Our God"
"How Can We Name a Love"
"In Thee Is Gladness"
"Jesus, Joy of Our Desiring"
"Joyful, Joyful, We Adore Thee"
"Let All the World in Every Corner Sing"
"Let's Sing to the Lord / Cantemos al Señor"
"Lord of All Hopefulness"
"Love Divine, All Loves Excelling"
"O God, Our Help in Ages Past"
"O Perfect Love"
"O Young and Fearless Prophet"
"Praise, My Soul, the King of Heaven"
"Praise the Lord Who Reigns Above"
"Praise to the Lord, the Almighty"
"Sing Praise to God Who Reigns Above"
"The King of Lord My Shepherd Is"
"Where Charity and Love Prevail"
"Where Love Is Found"
"Ye Watchers and Ye Holy Ones"
"Your Love, O God, Has Called Us Here"

During the service, other suggested hymns might include

"As Man and Woman We Were Made"
"Be Thou My Vision"

"Come, Christians, Join to Sing"
"Come, My Way, My Truth, My Life"
"O Lord, May Church and Home Combine"
"O Perfect Love"
"The Gift of Love"
"The King of Love My Shepherd Is"
"When Love Is Found"
"Where Charity and Love Prevail"
"Your Love, O God, Has Called Us Here"

A hymn may be sung or instrumental music played as the couple, the wedding party, and the people leave. Traditionally, this music might have included the "Wedding March" from Mendelssohn's music for A Midsummer Night's Dream. *The following recessional hymns may be chosen for the congregation to sing during the recessional:*

"All Praise to Thee, for Thou, O King Divine"
"Come We That Love the Lord"
"God, Whose Love Is Reigning o'er Us"
"Joyful, Joyful, We Adore Thee"
"Love Divine, All Loves Excelling"
"Now Thank We All Our God"
"Ye Watchers and Ye Holy Ones"

CHAPTER NINE
Scripture Lessons, Psalms, and Poetry

B*efore the Scripture lessons, the following prayer may be said:*

God of mercy,
    your faithfulness to your covenant frees us to live together
    in the security of your powerful love.
Amid the changing words of our generation,
    speak your eternal Word that does not change.
Then may we respond to your gracious promises
    by living in faith and obedience;
through our Lord Jesus Christ. **Amen.**   (Presbyterian)

One or more of the following Scripture lessons may be read by either the pastor or laypersons (such as members of the family or wedding party) as a witness to the Bible's affirmation of love and marriage. Other readings from popular literature or poetry may also be read. A hymn, psalm, canticle, anthem, or other music may be offered before or after the readings, during which the congregation may be invited to stand.

If there are lengthy readings or a homily, arrange for the wedding party to be seated at this time. Sometimes, these readings may be printed in the wedding bulletin so that persons may follow along.

The lessons are listed according to their order in the Bible.

Suggested Scripture Lessons

Genesis 1:26-28, 31a   The creation of man and woman
Genesis 2:4-10, 15-24   Becoming one flesh
Proverbs 3:3-6   A seal upon your heart

Song of Solomon 2:10-14, 16a; 8:6-7	Love is strong as death.
Isaiah 43:1-7	You are precious in God's eyes.
Isaiah 54:5-8	Your maker is your husband.
Isaiah 55:10-13	You shall go out in joy.
Isaiah 61:10–62:3	Exult in God.
Isaiah 63:7-9	The steadfast love of the Lord
Jeremiah 31:31-34	New covenant
Tobit 8:4-8	Good for man not to be alone
Matthew 5:1-10, 13-16	The Beatitudes
Matthew 7:21, 24-27	A house built upon a rock
Matthew 19:3-6	One flesh
Matthew 22:35-40	Love, the greatest commandment
Mark 2:18-22	Joy in Christ as at a wedding
Mark 10:6-9	No longer two but one
Mark 10:42-45	True greatness
John 2:1-11	The marriage feast of Cana
John 15:1-8	Bear good fruit.
John 15:9-17	Remain in Christ's love.
Romans 7:1-2, 9-18	Law and grace
Romans 12:1-2, 9-18	The life of a Christian
Romans 15:1-3, 5-7, 13	Live in harmony.
1 Corinthians 13	The greatest of these is love.
2 Corinthians 5:14-17	In Christ we are a new creation.
Ephesians 2:4-10	God's love for us
Ephesians 3:14-21	Be subject to one another.
Ephesians 4:1-6	Called to the one hope
Ephesians 4:25–5:2	Members one of another
Philippians 2:1-2	The Christlike spirit
Philippians 4:4-9	Rejoice in the Lord.
Colossians 3:12-17	Live in love and thanksgiving.
1 John 3:18-24	Love one another.
1 John 4:7-16	God is love.
Revelation 19:1, 5-9a	The wedding feast of the Lamb

Suggested Psalms

8	Crowed with glory and honor
23	The Lord is my shepherd.
33	Sing to the Lord a new song.
34	I will bless the Lord.
37	Trust in the Lord and do good.
67	May God be gracious to us.
100	Make a joyful noise to the Lord.
103	Bless the Lord, O my soul.
112	Happy are those who fear the Lord.
117	God's steadfast love
121	Lift up my eyes to the hills.
128	Blessed are those who fear the Lord.
145	The Lord is gracious.
148	Praise the Lord from the heavens.
150	Praise the Lord.

Following the Scripture lessons, psalm, and hymn, friends and family may speak briefly about marriage or the couple.

Another source of material to be read may come from classic or modern literature. A couple may choose the pastor or other participant to read a poem or short passage. Or either the groom or the bride may read a poem or literature to the other partner. Popular love poems have been some of William Shakespeare's 154 sonnets, especially 15, 25, 76, 88, 91, 115, and 126. Other couples like material from Kahlil Gibran, Robert Burns, John Keats, or another favorite poet or author.

CHAPTER TEN
Homily

A homily is a short sermon, witness, or biblical commentary by the presiding pastor or other leader of worship.

The homily may be a meditation on the Scripture or psalms read during the service. The homily brings together the word of God read with the couple and whole congregation.

This witness may also include some statement about the couple and their marriage, and a few words of wisdom to them. The homily might include what brought this couple together and how their personalities might complement each other. The homily may also speak about the setting of the wedding, the time of the year, or something else that makes this ceremony unique. For example, why did the couple choose to be married in this sanctuary or the particular setting?

The focus of the homily, however, should be the couple and the God who blesses their marriage. The pastor must be careful not to overwhelm or dominate the essential focus of the service: the uniting of the couple, the holding of hands, the exchanging of vows, the giving and receiving of rings, and the blessing upon the couple.

If the couple wishes to have a homily, speak to the pastor about what the homily might include.

CHAPTER ELEVEN
Intercessory Prayer

Following the reading of Scripture and the homily (if chosen), the pastor or other participant may offer one of the following prayers for the couple. These prayers serve as a bridge between the Scripture reading and the vows of the couple. These prayers may be printed in the wedding bulletin for the whole congregation to pray together.

11.1

Eternal God, Creator and Preserver of all life,
   Author of salvation, Giver of all grace:
Bless and sanctify with your Holy Spirit
   Groom's Name and *Bride's Name*, who come now to join in marriage.
Grant that they may give their vows to each other
   in the strength of your steadfast love.
Enable them to grow in love and peace
   with you and with one another all their days,
   that they may reach out
   in concern and service to the world;
   through Jesus Christ our Lord. **Amen.**   (United Methodist)

11.2

Eternal God, creator and preserver of all life,
   author of salvation, and giver of all grace:
Look with favor upon the world you have made,
   and for which your Son gave his life,
   and especially upon this man and this woman
   whom you make one flesh in Holy Matrimony. **Amen.**

Give them wisdom and devotion
     in the ordering of their common life,

that each may be to the other a strength in need,
a counselor in perplexity, a comfort in sorrow,
and a companion in joy. **Amen.**

Grant that their wills be so knit together in your will,
and their spirits in your Spirit,
that they may grow in love and peace with you
and one another all the days of their life. **Amen.**

Give them grace, when they hurt each other,
to recognize and acknowledge their faults,
and to seek each other's forgiveness and yours. **Amen.**

Make their life together a sign of Christ's love
to this sinful and broken world, that unity may overcome estrangement,
forgiveness heal guilt, and joy conquer despair. **Amen.**

Bestow on them, if it is your will, the gift and heritage of children,
and the grace to bring them up to know you,
to love you, and to serve you. **Amen.**

Give them such fulfillment of their mutual affection
that they may reach out in love and concern for others. **Amen.**

Grant that all married persons who have witnessed these vows
may find their lives strengthened
and their loyalties confirmed. **Amen.**

Grant that the bonds of our common humanity,
by which all your children are united one to another,
and the living to the dead, may be so transformed by your grace,
that your will may be done on earth as it is in heaven;
where, O Father, with your Son and the Holy Spirit,
you live and reign in perfect unity, now and forever. **Amen.**

(Episcopal)

11.3

Eternal God, without your grace no promise is sure.
Strengthen *Groom's Name* and *Bride's Name*
    with patience, kindness, gentleness,
   and all other gifts of your Spirit,
  so that they may fulfill the vows they have made.
Keep them faithful to each other and to you.
Fill them with such love and joy
   that they may build a home of peace and welcome.
Guide them by your Word to serve you all their days.
Help us all, O God,
   to do your will in each of our homes and lives.
Enrich us with your grace so that, supporting one another,
   we may serve those in need
   and hasten the coming of peace, love, and justice on earth,
through Jesus Christ our Lord. **Amen.**   (Presbyterian)

11.4

Gracious God, your generous love surrounds us,
   and everything we enjoy comes from you.
In your great love you have given us the gift of marriage.
Bless *Groom's Name* and *Bride's Name*
   as they pledge their lives to each other;
   that their love may continue to grow
   and be the true reflection of your love for us all;
through Jesus Christ our Lord. **Amen.**   (Australian)

11.5

Father, by your power you have made everything out of nothing.
In the beginning you created the universe
   and made humankind in your own likeness.
You gave man the constant help of woman
   so that man and woman should no longer be two,
     but one flesh,
   and you teach us that what you have united
     may never be divided.

Father, by your plan man and woman are united,
    and married life has been established
    as the one blessing that was not forfeited by original sin
    or washed away in the flood.
Look with love upon this woman, your daughter,
    now joined to her husband in marriage.
She asks your blessing.
Give her the grace of love and peace.
May she always follow the example of the holy women
    whose praises are sung in the scriptures.
May her husband put his trust in her
    and recognize that she is his equal
    and the heir with him to the life of grace.
May he always honor her and love her
    as Christ loves his bride, the Church.
Father, keep them always true to your commandments.
Keep them faithful in marriage
    and let them be living examples of Christian life.
Give them the strength which comes from the gospel
    so that they may be witnesses of Christ to others.
(Bless them with children
    and help them to be good parents.
May they live to see their children's children.)
And, after a happy old age,
    grant them fullness of life within the kingdom of heaven.
We ask this through Christ our Lord.   (Roman Catholic)

11.6

Holy Father, you created humankind in your own image
    and made man and woman to be joined as husband and wife
in union of body and heart,
    and so fulfill their mission in this world.
Father, to reveal the plan of your love,
    you made the union of husband and wife
    an image of the covenant between you and your people.
In the fulfillment of this sacrament [sign],

the marriage of Christian man and woman
is a sign of the marriage between Christ and the Church.
Father, stretch out your hand, and bless
    Groom's Name and *Bride's Name*.
Lord, grant that as they begin to live this sacrament [sign]
    they may share with each other the gifts of your love
    and become one in heart and mind
    as witnesses to your presence in their marriage.
Help them to create a home together
    (and give them children to be formed by the gospel
    and to have a place in your family).
Give your blessings to *Bride's Name*, your daughter,
    so that she may be a good wife (and mother),
    caring for the home, faithful in love for her husband,
    generous and kind.
Give your blessings to *Groom's Name*, your son,
    so that he may be a faithful husband (and a good father).
Father, grant that as they come together to your table on earth,
    so they may one day have the joy
        of sharing your feast in heaven.
We ask this through Christ our Lord.   (Roman Catholic)

11.7

Holy Father, creator of the universe,
    maker of man and woman in your own likeness,
    source of blessing for married life,
    we humbly pray to you for this woman
    who today is united with her husband
        in this sacrament of marriage.
May your fullest blessing come upon her and her husband
    so that they may together rejoice in your gift of married love
    (and enrich your Church with their children).
Lord, may they both praise you when they are happy
    and turn to you in their sorrows.
May they be glad that you help them in their work
    and know that you are with them in their need.

May they pray to you in the community of the Church,
    and be your witnesses in the world.
May they reach old age in the company of their friends,
    and come at last to the kingdom of heaven.
We ask this through Christ our Lord.   (Roman Catholic)

11.8

Almighty God, in whom we live and move and have our being,
    look graciously upon the world which you have made
    and for which your Son gave his life,
    and especially on all whom you make
        to be one flesh in holy marriage.

May their lives together be a sacrament
        of your love to this broken world,
    so that unity may overcome estrangement,
    forgiveness heal guilt, and joy overcome despair.
Lord, in your mercy, **Hear our prayer.**

May *Groom's Name* and *Bride's Name* so live together
    that the strength of their love
    may enrich our common life
    and become a sign of your faithfulness.
Lord, in your mercy, **Hear our prayer.**

May they receive the gift and heritage of children
    and the grace to bring them up to know and love you.
Lord, in your mercy, **Hear our prayer.**

May their home be a place of truth, security, and love;
    and their lives an example of concern for others.
Lord, in your mercy, **Hear our prayer.**

May those who have witnessed these vows find their lives strengthened
    and their loyalties confirmed.
Lord, in your mercy, **Hear our prayer.**   (Canadian Anglican)

CHAPTER TWELVE
Exchange of Vows

*T*his holy action is the heart of the wedding service, when the man and the woman declare publicly their commitment to each other. While the pastor may prompt the vows, the vows are spoken by and to the bride and the groom. In this sense, the couple themselves perform the wedding service, and everyone else is simply a witness. Alternatively, in Eastern Orthodox congregations, the vows are offered silently.

The couple should make sure that the vows made between them accurately reflect their own beliefs and values. In many services, this is the one place where couples make individual changes. The woman and the man face each other, joining hands, and speak to each other. When the groom speaks, he holds the bride's hands and speaks directly to her. When the bride speaks, she holds the groom's hands and speaks directly to him. The pastor may prompt them, line by line.

In speaking, the bridal couple should speak clearly so that the whole congregation may hear their vows to each other.

The bride typically gives her bridal bouquet to her maid/matron of honor prior to the Exchange of Vows, in order to free up both of her hands for the holding of hands and Exchange of Vows.

12.1

In the name of God,
I, *Name*, take you, *Name*, to be my wife/husband,
   to have and to hold
   from this day forward,
   for better, for worse,
   for richer, for poorer,
   in sickness and in health,
   to love and to cherish,
   until we are parted by death.
This is my solemn vow.   (United Methodist and Episcopal)

12.2

I take you, *Name,* to be my wife/husband,
 and I promise before God and all who are present here
 to be your loving and faithful husband/wife
 as long as we both shall live.
I will serve you with tenderness and respect,
 and encourage you to develop God's gifts in you.

             (United Methodist)

12.3

Name, in the name of God,
 I take you to be my husband/wife from this time onward,
 to join with you and to share all that is to come,
 to give and to receive,
 to speak and to listen,
 to inspire and to respond,
 and in all our life together
 to be loyal to you with my whole being,
 as long as we both shall live.   (United Methodist)

12.4

I, *Name,* take you, *Name,*
 to be my wedded wife/husband,
 to have and to hold,
 from this day forward,
 for better, for worse,
 for richer, for poorer,
 in sickness and in health,
 to love and to cherish,
 till death us do part,
 according to God's holy ordinance;
 and thereto I pledge you my faith.   (Methodist)

12.5

I take you, *Name,*
 to be my wife/husband from this day forward,

to join with you and share all that is to come,
and I promise to be faithful to you
until death parts us.

(Lutheran 1978)

12.6

In the presence of God and this community,
    I, *Name*, take you, Name, to be my wife/husband;
To have and to hold from this day forward,
    in joy and in sorrow,
    in plenty and in want,
    in sickness and in health,
    to love and to cherish,
    as long as both shall live.
This is my solemn vow.

(Lutheran 2006)

12.7

Name, I give myself to you to be your wife/husband.
I promise to love and sustain you in the covenant of marriage,
    from this day forward,
    in sickness and in health,
    in plenty and in want,
    in joy and in sorrow,
    as long as we both shall live.

(United Church of Christ)

12.8

I, *Name*, take you *Name*, to be my wife/husband;
    and I promise,
before God and these witnesses,
    to be your loving and faithful husband/wife;
in plenty and in want;
in joy and in sorrow;
in sickness and in health;
as long as we both shall live.

(Presbyterian)

12.9

Before God and these witnesses,
    I, *Name*, take you, *Name*, to be my wife/husband,
and I promise to love you,
and to be faithful to you,
as long as we both shall live.   (Presbyterian)

12.10

I, *Name*, take you, *Name*, to be my wife/husband,
    according to God's holy will.
I will love you,
    and share my life with you,
in sickness and in health,
in poverty and in prosperity,
in conflict and in harmony,
as long as we both shall live.
This is my solemn vow.   (Australian)

12.11

I, *Name*, in the presence of God,
    take you, *Name*, to be my wife/husband.
All that I am I give to you,
    and all that I have I share with you.
Whatever the future holds,
    I will love you and stand by you,
as long as we both shall live.
This is my solemn vow.   (Australian)

12.12

Man to woman:

I, *Name*, take thee, *Name*,
    to be my wife in Christian marriage.
I promise God,
    and I promise you that I will be Christian
        in my actions and attitudes.

I will serve the Lord with you;
   I will provide Christian leadership in our home.
I will work to meet our financial responsibilities;
   I will be faithful to you and to you alone.
I will weep with you in sorrow,
   rejoice with you in blessings,
   and be your faithful companion until Christ calls us home.
I make this vow to you, so help me God.

Woman to man:

I, *Name*, take thee, *Name*,
   to be my husband in the Lord.
I promise God, and I promise you that I will cherish you,
   I will obey you,
   I will love you,
   I will provide a shoulder to cry on,
   a heart that understands,
   a warm home for you to live in,
   and open arms for you to lean on.
I will pray for you and encourage you;
   I will weep when you weep,
   laugh when you laugh,
   and be yours and yours alone
      until our Lord separates us by death.
This I solemnly and joyfully promise,
   so help me God.   (Baptist)

12.13

I take you, as a gift from God,
   to be my lifelong companion
   through tears and laughter,
   sickness and health,
   work and play.
I will love you faithfully,
   constantly and prayerfully,
now and forever. Amen.   (Alternatives)

12.14

I promise to be faithful to you,
   open and honest with you.
I will respect, trust, help, and care for you.
I will share my life with you.
I will forgive you as we have been forgiven.
I will lead with you a simple, just, and peaceful life
   as Christ has called us to live.
And with you I will work
   to further simplicity, justice, and peace in our world.
I will love you
   and be thankful for the blessing of your love
   until death parts us.   (Alternatives)

12.15

Name, I commit myself to be with you
   in joy and adversity,
   in wholeness and brokenness,
   in peace and trouble,
   living with you in fidelity and love all our days.
         (United Church of Canada)

12.16

Name, I give myself to you in marriage
   and vow to be your husband/wife
   all the days of our lives.
I give you my hands
   and take your hands in mine
   as a symbol and pledge
   of our uniting in one flesh.
I give you my love,
   the outpouring of my heart,
   as a symbol and pledge
   of our uniting in one spirit.
I give you this ring
   from out of my worldly goods

as a symbol and pledge
of our uniting as one family.   (Reformed)

12.17

I take you, *Name,* to be my wife/husband from this day forward,
    to join with you and share all that is to come,
    and with the help of God
I promise to be faithful to you as God gives us life together.

(Evangelical Covenant)

12.18

Name, will you take *Name*
    to be your husband/wife,
to love, honor, and cherish him/her
    now and forevermore?
I will.   (Unitarian)

12.19

In the presence of God and these our Friends,
    I take thee to be my wife/husband,
promising with divine assistance
    to be unto thee a loving husband/wife
as long as we both shall live.   (Quaker)

CHAPTER THIRTEEN
Taking, Blessing, and Exchanging of Rings

*T*he wedding rings serve as a public witness and sacred sign that the man and woman are married. The use of wedding rings dates back at least to the Romans. The Romans made the ring out of iron and placed it on the third finger, which the Romans believed had a "vein of love" that ran directly to the heart. In the Middle Ages in England, the ring symbolized a down payment from the groom to the bride and a sign of good intent. Until the sixteenth century in England, the wedding ring was on the third finger of the right hand. In Eastern Orthodox congregations, the rings are blessed three times.

The bride and groom may also decide to give each other a special gift alongside or other than rings. A piece of jewelry or article of clothing may be shared with each other with an appropriate statement to the congregation about the meaning of the sign. Other signs may include a loop of rosary beads (a Mexican tradition), sips of sake (a Japanese tradition), or the giving of a mangalsutra (Church of South India).

It was traditional for only the man to give a ring to the woman, but today, most services include both the man and the woman giving and receiving rings. This pattern of two rings began after World War II. Traditionally, the bride's wedding ring is put on first and then the engagement ring so that the wedding ring will be closest to the heart. In those cases, the engagement ring is worn on the wedding day on the right hand and then put on the left hand after the wedding ring. In some cases, the wedding ring may simply go on the same finger that already has the engagement ring.

Choose a Blessing or a Vow for the Exchanging of Rings.

The pastor, taking the rings, says one of the following as a Blessing:

13.1
These rings [symbols]
are the outward and visible sign

of an inward and spiritual grace,
signifying to us the union
   between Jesus Christ and his Church.

Bless, O Lord, the giving of these rings [symbols],
that they who wear them may live in your peace
   and continue in your favor
   all the days of their life;
through Jesus Christ our Lord. **Amen.**   (United Methodist)

13.2

These rings [symbols]
are the outward and visible sign
   of an inward and spiritual grace,
signifying to all the uniting
    of *Groom's Name* and *Bride's Name* in holy marriage.

Bless, O Lord, the giving of these rings [symbols],
that they who wear them may live in your peace
   and continue in your favor
   all the days of their life;
through Jesus Christ our Lord. **Amen.**   (United Methodist)

13.3

The wedding ring is the outward and visible sign
   of an inward and spiritual grace,
signifying to all the uniting
   of this man and woman in holy matrimony,
   through the Church of Jesus Christ our Lord.

Bless, O Lord, the giving of these rings,
that they who wear them may abide in thy peace,
   and continue in thy favor;
through Jesus Christ our Lord. **Amen.**   (Methodist)

13.4

Bless, O Lord, this ring to be a sign of the vows
　　by which this man and this woman
　　　　have bound themselves to each other;
through Jesus Christ our Lord. **Amen.**　　　　　　　　　　(Episcopal)

13.5

By these symbols of covenant promise, Gracious God,
　　remind *Groom's Name* and *Bride's Name*
　　of your encircling love and unending faithfulness
　　that in all their life together
　　they may know joy and peace in one another. **Amen.**
　　　　　　　　　　　　　　　　(United Church of Christ)

13.6

Eternal God,
　　who in the time of Noah
　　　　gave us the rainbow as a sign of promise,
　　bless these symbols that they also may be signs of promises
　　　　fulfilled in lives of faithful loving;
　　through Jesus Christ our Savior. **Amen.**
　　　　　　　　　　　　　　　　(United Church of Christ)

13.7

By your blessing, O God,
　　may these rings be to *Groom's Name* and *Bride's Name*
　　symbols of unending love and faithfulness,
reminding them of the covenant they have made this day,
　　through Jesus Christ our Lord. **Amen.**　　　　　(Presbyterian)

13.8

Bless O Lord these rings.
Bless him/her who gives and bless her/him who wears,
　　and bless her/him who gives and him/her who wears,
　　that they may live together in love and harmony,
through Jesus Christ our Savior. **Amen.**
　　　　　　　　　　　　　　(African Methodist Episcopal)

13.9

Blessed are you, God of steadfast love,
  source of our joy and end of our hope.
Bless this ring (these rings) given and received
  that it (they) may be symbol of the vow and covenant
Groom's Name and *Bride's Name* have made this day,
  through Jesus Christ our Lord. **Amen.**   (Canadian Anglican)

13.10

Heavenly Father, source of everlasting love,
  revealed to us in Jesus Christ
and poured into our hearts through your Holy Spirit;
that love which many waters cannot quench,
  neither the floods drown;
that love which is patient and kind,
  enduring all things without end;
by your blessing, let these rings be
    to *Groom's Name* and *Bride's Name*
  symbols to remind them of the covenant made this day
through your grace in the love of your Son
  and in the power of your Spirit. **Amen.**

                                               (Church of England 2000)

13.11

In all ages and among all peoples,
  the ring has been a symbol of that which is measureless,
  a symbol of measureless, boundless devotion.
It is a circle;
  it has neither beginning nor ending.
A circle of precious gold,
  indicating the longevity of your love
  and the pricelessness of your devotion.   (Baptist, altered)

*While placing the ring on the third finger of the recipient's left hand, the giver may
say, prompted line by line by the pastor:*

13.1a

Name, I give you this ring
   as a sign of my vow,
and with all that I am,
   and all that I have, I honor you;
in the name of the Father,
   and of the Son, and of the Holy Spirit
(or in the name of God).

(United Methodist and Episcopal and Lutheran 2006)

13.2a

In token and pledge
   of our constant faith and abiding love,
with this ring I thee wed,
in the name of the Father,
   and of the Son,
   and of the Holy Spirit. **Amen.**   (Methodist)

13.3a

I give you this ring as a sign of my love and
      faithfulness.   (Lutheran 1978)

13.4a

Name, I give you this symbol as a sign of my love and
      faithfulness.

Response:

Name, I receive this symbol as a sign of our love and faithfulness.

(United Church of Christ)

13.5a

Name, I give you this ring as a sign of our covenant,
   in the name of the Father,
   and of the Son,
   and of the Holy Spirit. **Amen.**

Response:

I receive this ring as a sign of our covenant,
   in the name of the Father,
   and of the Son,
   and of the Holy Spirit. **Amen.**   (Presbyterian)

13.6a
With this ring I wed you,
   and I endow you with my worldly possessions,
in the name of the Father, and of the Son, and of the
      Holy Ghost. **Amen.**

(African Methodist Episcopal)

13.7a
I give you this ring
   as a sign of our marriage.
With my body I honor you,
   all that I am I give to you,
and all that I have I share with you,
   within the love of God,
Father, Son, and Holy Spirit.   (Church of England 2000)

13.8a
As a token of mutual fidelity and affection
   the rings are now given and received.
With this ring, I wed you
   and pledge you my love now and forever.   (Unitarian)

CHAPTER FOURTEEN
Unity Candle

---

*T*he unity candle is a recent addition to the wedding service, created by the commercial wedding industry (another item to rent from the florist or decorator), and has become another visible sign that the husband and wife have become one. Such a symbol should remain secondary, however, to the primary sign acts of holding hands, exchanging vows, and sharing rings.

If a unity candle is used, the two side candles representing the husband and wife are lighted first, often by the respective mothers or other members of the family, while the family is being seated at the beginning of the service.

The center candle representing the marriage is lighted after the Exchanging of Rings or some later point in the service. The side candles are not extinguished because both husband and wife retain their personal identities even as they are one in marriage.

During the lighting of the unity candle, music may be played or an anthem sung.

During the lighting, it often seems best if no words are spoken, so that the congregation may focus on the action of the lighting of the unity candle. Or the pastor may say one of the following:

14.1
Then the man said:
>"This at last is bone of my bones
>>and flesh of my flesh;
>this one shall be called Woman,
>>for out of Man this one was taken."

Therefore a man leaves his father and his mother
>and clings to his wife, and they become one flesh.

Genesis 2:23-24

14.2

Groom's Name and *Bride's Name* light the unity candle,
    symbolizing that in marriage they are no longer two people,
    but in Christ they become one flesh.   (Baptist)

14.3

The candle ceremony symbolizes the one-flesh principle
    in Christian marriage.
The two become one and treat each other
    as if they were a part of their own flesh.
The love that comes out of this unity is best described
    by Ruth's words to Naomi in the Old Testament:
"Do not press me to leave you
    or to turn back from following you!
Where you go, I will go;
    where you lodge, I will lodge; your people shall be my people,
    and your God my God.
Where you die, I will die—
    there will I be buried." (Ruth 1:16-17)
In Christ the two become one.   (Baptist)

CHAPTER FIFTEEN
Declaration of Marriage

The pastor now declares to the congregation that the couple is now husband and wife. The wife and husband hold hands, and the pastor may place a hand on their joined hands. The pastor may also wrap a stole, a colorful vestment worn by clergy as a sign of the pastor being yoked to Christ, around their joined hands as a sign of their union.

15.1
Pastor to couple:

You have declared your consent and vows
   before God and this congregation.
May God confirm your covenant
   and fill you both with grace.

Pastor to people:

Now that *Groom's Name* and *Bride's Name*
   have given themselves to each other by solemn vows,
   with the joining of hands,
   (and the giving and receiving of rings,)
I pronounce (announce to you) that they are husband and wife;
   in the name of the Father,
   and of the Son, and of the Holy Spirit.
Those whom God has joined together,
   let no one put asunder. **Amen**.

(United Methodist and Episcopal)

15.2
Forasmuch as *Groom's Name* and *Bride's Name*
   have consented together in holy wedlock,

and have witnessed the same before God and this company,
and thereto have pledged their faith each to the other,
and have declared the same
by joining hands and by giving and receiving rings;
I pronounce that they are husband and wife together,
in the name of the Father,
and of the Son,
and of the Holy Spirit.
Those whom God hath joined together,
let no one put asunder. **Amen.**   (Methodist)

15.3

Pastor: Groom's Name and *Bride's Name*,
by their promises before God
and in the presence of this congregation,
have bound themselves to one another as husband and wife.

People: **Blessed be the Father and the Son
and the Holy Spirit now and forever.**

Pastor: Those whom God has joined together
let no one put asunder.

All: **Amen.**   (Lutheran 1978)

15.4

Pastor to couple:

Groom's Name and *Bride's Name*,
you have committed yourselves to each other
in this joyous and sacred covenant.
Become one. Fulfill your promises.
Love and serve God, honor Christ and each other,
and rejoice in the power of the Holy Spirit.

Pastor to congregation:

By their promises, made before us this day,
    Groom's Name and *Bride's Name*
  have united themselves as husband and wife
    in sacred covenant.
Those whom God has joined together let no one
      separate.   (United Church of Christ)

15.5

Groom's Name and *Bride's Name*,
  you are husband and wife with the blessing of Christ's church.
Be merciful in all your ways, kind in heart, and humble in mind.
Accept life, and be most patient and tolerant with one another.
Forgive as freely as God has forgiven you.
And, above everything else, be truly loving.
Let the peace of Christ rule in your hearts,
  remembering that as members of one body
    you are called to live in harmony,
and never forget to be thankful for what God has done for you.
                      (United Church of Christ)

15.6

Hear the words of our Lord Jesus Christ:
  From the beginning of creation, God made them male and female.
For this reason a man shall leave his father and mother
  and be joined to his wife, and the two shall become one.
So they are no longer two but one.
  Let no one separate those whom God has joined together.   (Australian)

Following the Declaration of Marriage, the congregation may be invited to stand, and a doxology or other hymn may be sung as a sign of celebration and response to the marriage. The following hymns may be sung:

  "Praise to the Lord, the Almighty"
  "The Gift of Love"
  "When Love Is Found"

CHAPTER SIXTEEN
Blessing of the Marriage

The pastor prays for the couple and offers the church universal's blessing to the marriage. The husband and wife may kneel, or remain standing, as the pastor prays. Determine in the planning if there is a kneeling bench or pad for use by the couple, and thus whether they will kneel or stand. In some traditions, the pastor wraps the end of the pastor's stole around the couple's hands during this prayer.

16.1

O God,

you have so consecrated the covenant of Christian marriage
    that in it is represented
    the covenant between Christ and his Church.
Send therefore your blessing upon
      Groom's Name and *Bride's Name*,
    that they may surely keep their marriage covenant,
    and so grow in love and godliness together
    that their home may be a haven of blessing and peace;
through Jesus Christ our Lord. **Amen.**

(United Methodist and Episcopal)

16.2

Most gracious God,

we give you thanks for your tender love
    in making us a covenant people
    through our Savior Jesus Christ
    and for consecrating in his name
    the marriage covenant of *Groom's Name* and *Bride's Name*.
Grant that their love for each other
    may reflect the love of Christ for us

and grow from strength to strength
as they faithfully serve you in the world.
Defend them from every enemy.
Lead them into all peace.
Let their love for each other
be a seal upon their hearts,
a mantle about their shoulders,
and a crown upon their heads.
Bless them in their work and in their companionship;
in their sleeping and in their waking;
in their joys and in their sorrows;
in their lives and in their deaths.
Finally, by your grace,
bring them and all of us to that table
where your saints feast forever
in your heavenly home;
through Jesus Christ our Lord,
who with you and the Holy Spirit
lives and reigns,
one God, for ever and ever. **Amen.**

(United Methodist and Episcopal and Lutheran 2006)

16.3

O eternal God,
creator and preserver of us all,
giver of all spiritual grace,
the author of everlasting life:
Send thy blessing upon *Groom's Name* and *Bride's Name*,
whom we bless in thy name;
that they may surely perform and keep
the vow and covenant between them made,
and may ever remain in perfect love and peace together
and live according to thy laws.
Look graciously upon them,
that they may love, honor, and cherish each other,

and so live together in faithfulness and patience,
    in wisdom and true godliness,
that their home may be a haven of blessing
    and a place of peace;
through Jesus Christ our Lord. **Amen.**   (Methodist)

16.4

The Lord God,
    who created our first parents
      and established them in marriage,
establish and sustain you,
    that you may find delight in each other
and grow in holy love until your life's end. **Amen.**

(Lutheran 1978)

16.5

Let us bless God for all the gifts in which we rejoice today.
Lord God, constant in mercy, great in faithfulness:
With high praise we recall your acts of unfailing love
      for the human family,
    for the house of Israel, and for your people the Church.
We bless you for the joy which your servants,
     Groom's Name and *Bride's Name,*
    have found in each other,
and pray that you give to us such a sense of your constant love
    that we may employ all our strength in a life of praise of you,
whose work alone holds true and endures forever. **Amen.**

(Lutheran 1978)

16.6

Let us pray for *Groom's Name* and *Bride's Name*
     in their life together.
Faithful Lord, source of love,
    pour down your grace upon *Groom's Name* and *Bride's Name,*
that they may fulfill the vows they have made this day,

and reflect your steadfast love in their lifelong faithfulness
    to each other.
As members with them of the body of Christ,
    use us to support their life together;
and from your great store of strength
       give them power and patience,
    affection and understanding, courage and love
toward you, toward each other, and toward the world,
that they may continue together in mutual growth
according to your will in Jesus Christ our Lord. **Amen.**

(Lutheran 1978)

16.7

The grace of Christ attend you;
    the love of God surround you;
    the Holy Spirit keep you that you may grow in holy love,
    find delight in each other always,
    and remain faithful until your life's end. **Amen.**

(United Church of Christ)

16.8

May the God of Sarah and Abraham,
    who watches over all the families of the earth,
    bless your new family and establish your home in peace
       and steadfast love. **Amen.**

(United Church of Christ)

16.9

Merciful God, we thank you for your love that lives within us
    and calls us from loneliness to companionship.
We thank you for all who have gone before us:
    for Adam and Eve, for Sarah and Abraham,
       for Joseph and Mary,
    and for countless parents whose names we do not know.
We thank you for our own parents,
    and for all, whether married or single,

who are mother or father to us, as we grow to the fullness
of the stature of Christ.
Bless *Groom's Name* and *Bride's Name*,
that they may have the grace
to live the promises they have made.
Defend them from all enemies of their love.
Teach them the patience of undeserved forgiveness.
Bring them to old age,
rejoicing in love's winter
more fully than in its springtime. **Amen.**

(United Church of Christ)

16.10

Pastor: Blessed are you, heavenly Father:

People: **You give joy to bridegroom and bride.**

Pastor: Blessed are you, Lord Jesus Christ:

People: **You have brought new life to the world.**

Pastor: Blessed are you, Holy Spirit of God:

People: **You bring us together in love.**

Pastor: Blessed be Father, Son, and Holy Spirit:

People: **One God to be praised forever. Amen.**   (Australian)

16.11

In peace, let us pray to the Lord:
All grace comes from you, O God,
and you alone are the source of eternal life.
Bless your servants *Groom's Name* and *Bride's Name*,
that they may faithfully live together to the end of their lives.
May they be patient and gentle, ready to trust each other,

and to face together the challenge of the future.
May they pray together in joy and in sorrow,
    and always give thanks for the gift of each other.
Be with them in all their happiness;
    that your joy may be in them, and their joy may be full.
Strengthen them in every time of trouble,
    that they may bear each other's burdens,
    and so fulfill the law of Christ.
Give *Groom's Name* and *Bride's Name* grace,
    when they hurt each other,
    to recognize and acknowledge their fault,
    to ask each other's forgiveness,
    and to know your mercy and love.
May your peace dwell in their home,
    and be a sign of hope for peace in the world.
Let their home be a place of welcome,
    that its happiness may be freely shared.
Through loving one another in Christ,
    may they be strengthened to love Christ in their neighbor.
May they be creative in their daily work,
    and find fulfillment in the life of their community.

(One of the following two prayers may be included.)
May *Groom's Name* and *Bride's Name*
        enjoy the gift and heritage of children.
Grant that they may be loving and wise parents,
    with grace to bring up their children
    to know you, to love you, and to serve you.

or

May *Groom's Name* and *Bride's Name*
        enjoy the gift and heritage of their children.
Grant them the grace to share their love and faith
    with *Names of Children*
that they may grow together as a loving family.

Bless the parents and families
   of *Groom's Name* and *Bride's Name*,
  that they may be united in love and friendship.
Grant that all married people
  who have witnessed these vows today
  may find their lives strengthened
  and their loyalties confirmed.
We ask these prayers in the name of Christ our Lord. **Amen.**

(Australian)

16.12

Almighty and most merciful God,
  who has now united this man and this woman
     in the holy estate of matrimony,
  grant them grace to live therein according to your holy word.
Strengthen them in constant fidelity
     and true affection toward each other;
  sustain and defend them amid all the trials and temptations,
     and help them so to pass through this world
        in faith toward you,
  in communion with your holy church,
     and in loving service one of the other
  that they may enjoy forever your heavenly benediction,
through Jesus Christ, your Son, our Lord,
  who lives and reigns with you and the Holy Ghost,
  ever One God, world without end. **Amen.**

(African Methodist Episcopal)

16.13

Almighty God,
  you send your Holy Spirit
     to be the life and light of all your people.
Open the hearts of these your children to the riches of his grace,
  that they may bring forth the fruit of the Spirit
  in love and joy and peace
through Jesus Christ our Lord. **Amen.**   (Church of England 1980)

16.14

Heavenly Father, maker of all things,
    you enable us to share in your work of creation.
Bless this couple in the gift and care of children,
    that their home may be a place of love, security, and truth,
    and their children grow up to know and love you
in your Son Jesus Christ our Lord. **Amen.**

(Church of England 1980)

16.15

Lord and Savior Jesus Christ,
    who shared at Nazareth the life of an earthly home:
    reign in the home of these your servants as Lord and King;
    give them grace to minister to others
        as you have ministered to all persons,
    and grant that by deed and word
        they may be witnesses of your saving love
    to those among whom they live;
    for the sake of your holy name. **Amen.**

(Church of England 1980)

16.16

Pastor: All grace comes from you, O God,
    and you alone are the source of eternal life.
Bless your servants *Groom's Name* and *Bride's Name,*

People: **that they may faithfully live together
    to the end of their lives.**

Pastor: Be with them in all their happiness

People: **that your joy may be in them,
    and their joy may be full.**

Pastor: Strengthen them in every time of trouble

People: **that they may carry each other's burdens
and so fulfill the law of Christ.**

Pastor: Let your blessing be on their home

People: **that your peace may dwell there.**

Pastor: Let it be a place of welcome

People: **that its happiness may be freely shared.**

Pastor: Bless the families and friends
of *Groom's Name* and *Bride's Name*

People: **that we may be united in love and friendship.**

Pastor: Now to him who is able to keep you from falling
and to present you faultless
before the presence of his glory with rejoicing,

People: **to the only God, our Savior,
through Jesus Christ our Lord,
be glory, majesty, dominion and authority,
both now and forever. Amen.**

(British Methodist)

16.17

May there be truth and understanding between you.
May you enjoy length of days,
fulfillment of hopes, and peace and contentment of mind.
May God bless and keep you always.

(United Church of Canada)

16.18

Most merciful and gracious God,
of Whom the whole family in heaven and earth is named,

we thank Thee for the love with which Thou dost bind
kindred souls together,
and especially for the institution of marriage,
the tenderness of its ties,
the honor of its estate,
and the sacredness of its obligations.
Look with favor upon these Thy servants;
sanctify and bless their union;
grant them grace to fulfill, with pure and steadfast affection,
the vow and covenant made between them.
Guide them together, we pray,
in the way of righteousness and peace,
that, loving and serving Thee,
with one heart and mind, all the days of their life,
they may be abundantly enriched by Thy grace.
Vouchsafe unto them the guidance of Thy Holy Spirit,
and teach them to do that which is well pleasing in Thy sight,
through Jesus Christ, our Lord. **Amen.** (Moravian)

16.19

O God, you have so consecrated the covenant of marriage
that in it is represented the spiritual unity
between Christ and his Church;
Send therefore your blessing upon these your servants,
that they may so love, honor, and cherish each other
in faithfulness and patience, in wisdom and true godliness,
that their home may be a haven of blessing and peace;
through Jesus Christ our Lord,
who lives and reigns with you and the Holy Spirit,
one God, now and forever. **Amen.** (Episcopal)

16.20

Faithful God, holy and eternal,
source of life and spring of love,
we thank and praise you for bringing
Groom's Name and *Bride's Name* to this day
and we pray for them.

Lord of life and love: **hear our prayer.**
May their marriage be life-giving and lifelong,
   enriched by your presence and strengthened by your grace;
may they bring comfort and confidence to each other
   in faithfulness and trust.
Lord of life and love: **hear our prayer.**
May the hospitality of their home
   bring refreshment and joy to all around them;
may their love overflow to neighbors in need
   and embrace those in distress.
Lord of life and love: **hear our prayer.**
May they discern in your word
   order and purpose for their lives;
and may the power of your Holy Spirit
   lead them in truth and defend them in adversity.
Lord of life and love: **hear our prayer.**

(Church of England 2000)

16.21

This prayer may also be added to any of the other prayers.
Pastor for children of new marriage:
Bless this child/these children,
   that he/she/they may find in this new home
      a haven of love and joy
where Jesus Christ is honored in kind words and tender deeds.

(United Church of Christ)

16.22

This prayer may also be added to any of the other prayers.

Pastor for all families:
Gracious Father, you bless family life and renew your people.
Enrich husbands and wives, parents and children
      more and more with your grace,
   that, strengthening and supporting each other,
   they may serve those in need
      and be a sign of the fulfillment of your kingdom,

where, with your Son Jesus Christ and the Holy Spirit,
you live and reign, one God through all ages. **Amen**.

(Australian)

At the end of the prayer, the pastor invites the congregation to pray the Lord's Prayer (see in chapter 17 three different forms of the Lord's Prayer).

A Filipino tradition is for the couple to feed each other cooked rice at this time. At an Armenian wedding two white doves are released as signs of love and happiness. A traditional Greek wedding would here include placing crowns of orange blossoms (signs of purity and loveliness) on the heads of the couple.

CHAPTER SEVENTEEN
The Lord's Prayer

The Lord's Prayer, the most important prayer that Jesus Christ taught his disciples, may be prayed by everyone, using one of the forms below. The wife and husband may continue to kneel (traditional) or may stand. Or the Lord's Prayer may be sung by a soloist or as a hymn by the congregation. Or the prayer may be offered following the Prayer of Thanksgiving if Holy Communion is served. If the congregation is praying the prayer together, be sure to indicate which translation will be used.

17.1
ECUMENICAL TEXT *(A contemporary version adopted by most English language liturgical traditions for public use.)*

Our Father in heaven, hallowed be your name,
   your kingdom come, your will be done, on earth as in heaven.
Give us today our daily bread.
Forgive us our sins as we forgive those who sin against us.
Save us from the time of trial and deliver us from evil.
For the kingdom, the power, and the glory are yours
   now and forever. **Amen.**

17.2
TRADITIONAL TEXT #1 *(A traditional version used in some Protestant congregations. Notice the use of* trespasses.*)*

Our Father, who art in heaven, hallowed be thy name.
Thy kingdom come, thy will be done, on earth as it is in heaven.
Give us this day our daily bread.
And forgive us our trespasses
   as we forgive those who trespass against us.

And lead us not into temptation, but deliver us from evil.
For thine is the kingdom, and the power, and the glory,
   forever. **Amen**.

17.3

TRADITIONAL TEXT #2 *(Another traditional version used in some Protestant congregations. Notice the use of debts.)*

Our Father, who art in heaven, hallowed be thy Name;
   thy kingdom come, thy will be done,
      on earth as it is in heaven.
Give us this day our daily bread;
   and forgive us our debts
   as we forgive our debtors;
and lead us not into temptation, but deliver us from evil.
For thine is the kingdom and the power and the glory,
   forever. **Amen.**

CHAPTER EIGHTEEN
Thanksgiving and Holy Communion

Holy Communion may be celebrated as the first act of the married couple. This Holy Meal remembers and reenacts Jesus Christ's meal with his disciples on the night before his death, and Jesus' meals with his disciples after his resurrection like that meal on the day of Easter at Emmaus and Jesus with his friends beside the Sea of Galilee.

This highest act of Christian worship is not a mournful or somber ritual, but a celebrative moment recognizing God's love. If the Lord's Supper is a part of the service, it is most important that the meal is included in a ceremony that includes the reading of Scripture. Also, not only the husband and wife but the whole congregation should be invited to receive the bread and cup of Holy Communion.

One reason why the meal often is not celebrated at a Christian wedding has to do with some traditions' limits on who may receive the bread and share the cup. The tradition of The United Methodist Church and The United Church of Christ, among other denominations, is to invite all Christians and even all people to the Lord's Table. Other traditions, however, may limit who may receive (for example, non–Roman Catholics may not receive at a Roman Catholic service where a priest presides). Finally, there should be no pressure that would embarrass those who for whatever reason do not choose to receive Holy Communion.

The husband and wife, or children from previous marriages, or representatives of the congregation may bring bread and wine/cup to the Lord's Table at this time if the elements of Holy Communion are not already on the table.

The pastor, standing if possible behind the Lord's Table, facing the people from this time through Breaking the Bread, takes the bread and cup; and the bread and wine are prepared for the meal.

The bread and wine are given first to the couple and then to the people. The new husband and wife may assist in the distribution.

While the bread and cup are given, the congregation may sing hymns, or there may be vocal or instrumental music.

The pastor will probably choose the appropriate prayer at the table, according to one's own tradition. The following prayers are two examples of Prayers of Great Thanksgiving at the Lord's Table.

18.1

The Lord be with you.
And also with you.
Lift up your hearts.
We lift them up to the Lord.
Let us give thanks to the Lord our God.
It is right to give our thanks and praise.

It is right, and a good and joyful thing,
   always and everywhere to give thanks to you,
    Father Almighty (almighty God),
      Creator of heaven and earth.
You formed us in your image, male and female you created us.
You gave us the gift of marriage, that we might fulfill each other.
And so,
   with your people on earth and all the company of heaven
   we praise your name and join their unending hymn:

Holy, holy, holy Lord, God of power and might,
heaven and earth are full of your glory.
   Hosanna in the highest.
Blessed is he who comes in the name of the Lord.
   Hosanna in the highest.

Holy are you, and blessed is your Son Jesus Christ.
By the baptism of his suffering, death, and resurrection
   you gave birth to your Church,
   delivered us from slavery to sin and death,
   and made with us a new covenant
   by water and the Spirit,

from which flows the covenant love of husband and wife.
On the night in which he gave himself up for us,
    he took bread, gave thanks to you, broke the bread,
    gave it to his disciples, and said:
"Take, eat; this is my body which is given for you.
Do this in remembrance of me."
When the supper was over he took the cup,
    gave thanks to you, gave it to his disciples, and said:
"Drink from this, all of you;
    this is my blood of the new covenant,
    poured out for you and for many
    for the forgiveness of sins.
Do this, as often as you drink it,
    in remembrance of me."
And so,
in remembrance of these your mighty acts in Jesus Christ,
we offer ourselves in praise and thanksgiving
    as a holy and living sacrifice,
    in union with Christ's offering for us,
as we proclaim the mystery of faith:

Christ has died; Christ is risen; Christ will come again.

Pour out your Holy Spirit on us gathered here,
    and on these gifts of bread and wine.
Make them be for us the body and blood of Christ,
that we may be for the world the body of Christ,
    redeemed by his blood.
By the same bless *Groom's Name* and *Bride's Name*,
that their love for each other
    may reflect the love of Christ for us
    and grow from strength to strength
    as they faithfully serve you in the world.
Defend them from every enemy.
Lead them into all peace.
Let their love for each other

be a seal upon their hearts,
a mantle about their shoulders,
and a crown upon their heads.
Bless them
in their work and in their companionship;
in their sleeping and in their waking;
in their joys and in their sorrows;
in their lives and in their deaths.
Finally, by your grace,
bring them and all of us to that table
where your saints feast forever in your heavenly home.
Through your Son Jesus Christ,
with the Holy Spirit in your holy Church,
all honor and glory is yours, almighty Father (God),
now and forever. **Amen**. (United Methodist)

18.2
The Lord be with you.
And also with you.
Lift up your hearts.
We lift them up to the Lord.
Let us give thanks to the Lord our God.
It is right to give our thanks and praise.

Blessed are you, O God our Creator.
From the womb of your being you brought forth worlds.
Into mere dust you blew the breath of life,
creating women and men to bear your likeness in the world.
You create, love, and care for all that is.
We praise you and thank you, nurturing God,
that in Jesus you bring joy and hope to loving hearts,
and offer health and power to human relationships.
Even the powers of sorrow and death
could not contain Christ's joy.
From the tomb our risen Savior came
to share bread again among the beloved.

In the glory of your banquet hall,
   Christ prepares a wedding feast for all the faithful
     who even now praise you.

Holy, holy, holy, God of love and majesty;
The whole universe speaks of your glory,
   O God Most High.
Blessed is the one who comes in the name of our God!
   Hosanna in the highest!

Merciful God,
   we remember that on the night of betrayal and desertion,
   Jesus took bread, gave thanks to you, broke the bread,
   and gave it to the disciples saying:
"Take, eat; this is my body broken for you."
Likewise, Jesus took the cup of blessing and said:
"Drink of this cup. It is the new covenant in my blood,
   poured out for you and for many for the forgiveness of sins.
Do this in memory of me."
With joy we thank you, God of gladness and warmth,
   that at Pentecost you sent your Holy Spirit
   to dance about the heads of your people,
   enabling your word to be heard afresh.
Now send your Holy Spirit
   on these gifts of bread and wine on us
   that we may be set afire with your love
    and leap with joy at your presence.
Pour out your blessing on *Groom's Name* and *Bride's Name*.
May they sing a new song of your great love
   in communion with you
    and all your saints in heaven and on earth.
May their love for each other proclaim
   the love of Christ for all of us.
May the faithful service of all your people
   bring peace, justice, joy, and love to all the world;

through Christ, with Christ, and in Christ,
  in the unity of the Holy Spirit,
all glory and honor are yours, Holy God,
    now and forever. **Amen**.

(United Church of Christ)

The Lord's Prayer may then be prayed (see chapter 17). All who wish or are able now receive the bread and cup, beginning with the couple.
  When all have received, the Lord's Table is put in order by the pastor.
  The pastor may offer one of the following prayers after Holy Communion:

18.3

Eternal God, we give you thanks
that you have brought *Groom's Name* and *Bride's Name*
    (and their families and friends)
  together at the table of your family.
Help them grow in love and unity,
that they may rejoice together all the days of their lives
  and in the wedding feast of heaven.
Grant this through Jesus Christ our Lord. **Amen.**

(United Methodist)

18.4

O God, the giver of all that is true and lovely and gracious;
We give you thanks for binding us together
  in these holy mysteries of the Body and Blood
    of your Son Jesus Christ.
Grant that by your Holy Spirit,
    Groom's Name and *Bride's Name*,
  now joined in Holy Matrimony,
  may become one in heart and soul, live in fidelity and peace,
and obtain those eternal joys prepared for all who love you;
for the sake of Jesus Christ our Lord. **Amen.**

(Episcopal)

18.5

Thank you, O God, for refreshing us at your table.
By your grace you have nourished us
   with the living presence of Christ, the bread of life,
   that we may share life together.
Send us forth in the power of your Holy Spirit
   to give ourselves in love until your entire human family
     is gathered at your table,
glorifying and praising you in the name of Jesus Christ. **Amen.**

(United Church of Christ)

18.6

Loving God, we thank you that you have fed us
   in this holy meal,
  united us with Christ,
and given us a foretaste of the marriage feast of the Lamb.
So strengthen us in your service
   that our daily living may show our thanks,
through Jesus Christ our Lord. **Amen.**   (Presbyterian)

CHAPTER NINETEEN
Dismissal with Blessing

---

*T*he service is almost over, and the pastor sends out the couple and congregation
to serve God and one another. In Eastern Orthodox congregations, this is where
the priest will lead the rite of the Crowning, the Cup, and the Triumphal Procession
of Isaiah. Here the congregation may sing a hymn or offer a psalm (see chapters 8,
"Hymns and Special Music," and 9, "Scripture Lessons, Psalms, and Poetry")
before the pastor offers one of the following final blessings for the couple and the
congregation.

19.1
Pastor to wife and husband:

God the Eternal keep you in love with each other,
   so that the peace of Christ may abide in your home.
Go to serve God and your neighbor in all that you do.

Pastor to people:

Bear witness to the love of God in this world,
   so that those to whom love is a stranger
      will find in you generous friends.
The grace of the Lord Jesus Christ,
   and the love of God,
   and the communion of the Holy Spirit
   be with you all. **Amen.**   (United Methodist)

19.2
God the Father, the Son, and the Holy Spirit
   bless, preserve, and keep you;

the Lord graciously with his favor look upon you,
and so fill you with all spiritual benediction and love
   that you may so live together in this life
   that in the world to come you may have life everlasting.
     Amen. (Methodist)

19.3

Almighty God, Father, Son, and Holy Spirit,
   keep you in his light and truth and love
     now and forever. **Amen.** (Lutheran 1978)

19.4

The blessed and holy Trinity
   make you strong in faith and love,
defend you on every side,
   and guide you in truth and peace,
now and forever. **Amen.** (Lutheran 2006)

19.5

God Almighty
   send your light and truth to keep you all the days of your life.
The hand of God protect you;
the holy angels accompany you;
and the blessings of almighty God,
   the Father, the Son, and the Holy Spirit,
be with you now and forever. **Amen.** (Lutheran 2006)

19.6

Go forth in the love of God;
   go forth in hope and joy, knowing
     that God is with you always.
And the peace of God which passes all understanding,
   keep your hearts and minds
     in the knowledge and love of God and of Jesus Christ;
and the blessing of God, Creator, Redeemer, and Sanctifier,
be with you, and remain with you always. **Amen.**

(United Church of Christ)

19.7
May God bless you and keep you.
May God's face shine upon you and be gracious to you.
May God look upon you with kindness and give you
      peace. **Amen.**

(United Church of Christ)

19.8
As God's own, clothe yourselves
      with compassion, kindness, and patience,
   forgiving each other as the Lord has forgiven you,
and crown all these things with love,
    which binds everything together in perfect harmony.

(Presbyterian)

19.9
Whatever you do, in word or deed,
   do everything in the name of the Lord Jesus,
giving thanks to God through him. (Presbyterian)

19.10
The grace of Christ attend you,
    the love of God surround you,
    the Holy Spirit keep you,
that you may live in faith, abound in hope, and grow in love,
    both now and forevermore. **Amen.** (Presbyterian)

19.11
God the Father, God the Son, God the Holy Spirit,
   bless, preserve, and keep you;
the Lord mercifully with his favor look upon you,
   and fill you with all spiritual benediction and grace;
that you may faithfully live together in this life,
    and in the age to come have life everlasting. **Amen.**

(Episcopal)

19.12
May God and your marriage bring you joy.
God give you joy of one another.   (Celtic)

19.13
Be ever in the embrace of the Father.
Be ever in the embrace of the Son.
Be ever in the embrace of the Spirit.
Be ever in the embrace of one another.   (Celtic)

19.14
May the Lord tie a bond of your love
　between you forever without loosening.   (Celtic)

19.15
The compassing of God be upon you,
　the compassing of the God of life.
The compassing of Christ be upon you,
　the compassing of the Christ of love.
The compassing of the Spirit be upon you,
　the compassing of the Spirit of grace.
The compassing of the Sacred Three be upon you,
　the compassing of the Sacred Three protect you,
　the compassing of the Sacred Three preserve you. **Amen.**

                                                                   (Celtic)

CHAPTER TWENTY
Introduction of the Couple

---

*T*he couple may greet each other with a kiss as the pastor says,

You may kiss.

Then, the couple may be introduced to the congregation by the pastor saying one of the following:

20.1
It is my privilege to introduce to you Mr. and Mrs. John Joe Smith (*groom's full name*).

20.2
I introduce to you John Joe Smith (*groom's full name*) and Jane Marie Doe (*bride's full name*), a couple together in the eyes of God.

20.3
I am pleased to introduce you to Mr. and Mrs. John and Jane Smith.

A hymn may be sung or instrumental music played as the couple, the wedding party, and the congregation leave. Traditionally, this music might have included Mendelssohn's "Wedding March." The following recessional hymns may be chosen for the congregation to sing during the recessional:

"All Praise to Thee, for Thou, O King Divine"
"Come We That Love the Lord"

"God, Whose Love Is Reigning o'er Us"
"Joyful, Joyful, We Adore Thee"
"Love Divine, All Loves Excelling"
"Now Thank We All Our God"
"Ye Watchers and Ye Holy Ones"

Be clear about when the pastor invites the congregation to stand and leave the worship space. Some grandparents and older family members may remain in the space for pictures after the wedding. Will persons be escorted out by pew or at their own discretion?

Also, be clear with the wedding party about pictures following the wedding. Should everyone immediately return to the worship space for pictures, or will there be a receiving line? Avoid confusion by making some clear decisions before the wedding and communicating this information to everyone at the rehearsal.

Acknowledgments

African Methodist Episcopal; the A.M.E. Sunday School Union.

Alternatives; Margaret and Mark Yackel-Juleen and Donna Rose-Heim. Used with permission.

Australian; from *An Australian Prayer Book* © Anglican Church of Australia Trust Corporation. Reproduced with permission.

Baptist; from *The Wedding Collection* by Morris Chapman. © 1991 Broadman Press. All rights reserved. Used by permission.

British Methodist; © The Methodist Conference 1974. Used by permission of the Methodist Publishing House.

Canadian Anglican; from *The Book of Alternative Services* of the Anglican Church of Canada, published by the Anglican Book Centre 1985. Used with permission.

Celtic; from *Celtic Daily Prayer: Prayers and Readings from the Northumbria Community,* Copyright © 2002 The Northumbria Community Trust Ltd.

Church of England 1980; with permission of the Central Board of Finance of the Church of England.

Church of England 2000; with permission of the Archbishop's Council of the Church of England 2000.

Church of Scotland; the Church of Scotland.

Church of South India; from the *Book of Common Worship of the Church of South India,* © Oxford University Press.

Ecumenical; © 1987 Hans Boehringer for the Consultation on Common Texts as found in *A Christian Celebration of Marriage*.

Episcopal; although copyright permission is not required for use of items from *The Book of Common Prayer, 1979,* as a courtesy, we acknowledge this source.

Evangelical Covenant; © Covenant Publications, 1981.

Evangelical United Brethren; © 1992 United Methodist Publishing House, 201 8th Avenue South, Nashville, TN 37203.

Lutheran 1978; reprinted from *Lutheran Book of Worship,* copyright © 1978, by permission of Augsburg Fortress.

Lutheran 2006; from Evangelical Lutheran Worship, copyright © 2006, by permission of Augsburg Fortress. Approved for worship in the Evangelical Lutheran Church in Canada and commended for use in the Evangelical Lutheran Church in America.

Methodist; © 1992 United Methodist Publishing House, 201 8th Avenue South, Nashville, TN 37203.

Moravian; from *Moravian Book of Worship,* 1995. Used by permission.

Presbyterian; from *Book of Common Worship.* © 1993 Westminster/John Knox Press. Used by permission of Westminster/John Knox Press.

Quaker; from a Quaker wedding attended by the author.

Reformed; *Worship the Lord,* James R. Esther and Donald J. Bruggink, editors. Copyright 1987 by the Board of Education of the Reformed Church in America. Used with permission.

Roman Catholic; excerpts from the English translation of *Rite of Marriage* © 1969, International Committee on English in the Liturgy, Inc. (ICEL); excerpts from the English translation of *The Roman Missal* © 1973, ICEL; excepts from *The Sacramentary* © 1985, Liturgical Press. All rights reserved.

Unitarian; from a Unitarian Universalist service attended by the author.

United Church of Canada; used by permission of the United Church of Canada.

United Church of Christ; adapted from *Book of Worship United Church of Christ* © 1986 United Church of Christ, Office for Church Life and Leadership, New York. Used by permission.

United Methodist; *A Service of Christian Marriage I,* from *The United Methodist Book of Worship.* © 1992 United Methodist Publishing House. Used by permission.